Keep the Faith, Baby!

To my mother, whose laughter is the most glorious sound I have ever heard.
To my wife, Ina, and children, Gillian, John, William, David and Nicola.
And to the numerous friends, colleagues and supporters whose good wishes, prayers, practical support and expectations continue to sustain me.

KEEP THE FAITH, BABY!

Wilfred Wood

Published by
The Bible Reading Fellowship
Peter's Way
Sandy Lane West
Oxford
OX4 5HG
ISBN 0 7459 2965 6
Albatross Books Pty Ltd
PO Box 320
Sutherland
NSW 2232
Australia
ISBN 0 7324 0901 2

First edition 1994

Acknowledgments

Extract from *The Heart of a Woman* on pages 50–51 copyright © 1981 by Maya Angelou. Published by Virago Press Limited.

A catalogue record for this book is available from the British Library

Printed and bound in Great Britain by Cox and Wyman Ltd, Reading

CONTENTS

EDITOR'S FOREWORD

This book is being published in July 1994 to coincide with the Black Anglican Congress being held in the ancient cathedral city of York in England. Hundreds of delegates from all over Britain will gather together in a celebration for the Decade of Evangelism.

The Committee on Black Anglican Concerns had six objectives in planning the congress.

1. To recognize, celebrate and rejoice in the diversity of gifts which black Anglicans bring to the Church.

2. To devise ways and means of encouraging young black Anglicans to remain and become involved in the Church at all levels.

3. To plan strategies towards using the gifts of black Anglicans in the tasks of evangelism.

4. To help black Anglicans develop confidence and leadership potential, and to offer this confidence as a gift to the whole Church.

5. To discuss the progress of dioceses towards implementing recommendations from *Seeds of Hope*, the Report of a survey on combating racism in the Dioceses of the Church of England which was published in 1991.

6. To encourage the Church to live the Christian faith authentically and therefore to confront society in areas of racial injustices.

They end their statement of objectives by saying that 'Evangelism and caring go hand in hand: the gospel needs demonstrating as well as proclaiming.'

The Committee hopes that the event will stimulate the process of: reflection and celebration, confidence building, renewed commitment, decision making, mission and evangelism, and unity.

The Archbishops of Canterbury and York will be present at the Congress, and all the Diocesan Bishops have been invited, together with members of the General Synod's Standing Committee and the Chairpersons and Secretaries of their Boards and Councils. These will be involved 'as listeners, as participants in dialogue, and also in effective solidarity, decision making and action'. Observers from other churches as well as church-based organizations have also been invited.

The Congress will end with the celebration of the Eucharist in York Minister. The celebrant will be the Archbishop of York and the preacher will be Bishop Wilfred Wood.

It was his idea to put this book together, and he invited me to work on it with him. Over the years he has spoken many times on race relations, on the faith, on community and on evangelism—so he and I have looked at the material and selected, edited and shaped it into *Keep the Faith, Baby!*

This book is about being a Christian and also about being black. It is an essential read for all Christians, brown and beige and yellow as well as black—and for Baptists, Pentcostals, Methodists, Congregationalists and all the other denominations in Christ's beloved but divided Church.

'God so loved the *world* that he gave his one and only Son, that whoever believes in him shall not perish but have eternal life. For God did not send his Son into the world to condemn the world, but to save the world through him' (John 3:16–17, NIV)

To be 'saved' is to come into a living relationship with the living God whose name and whose character is love. If you and I are Christians then our sins are forgiven, and as we confess and repent of them they will go on being forgiven, because God loves us and Christ died for us. Then we shall go out to God's beloved world in the power of the Holy Spirit to love the people in it and to forgive them as God in Christ has forgiven us.

But if we don't love our neighbour, whatever colour she is, or whatever ethnic group he belongs to, then there is an enormous question mark over the reality of our relationship with the God of love.

It is good and timely that this book is being published in Britain at this time, since earlier this year the media reported the arrival here of that evil organization called the Ku Klux Klan. May God help us to overcome evil with good and hate with love. This book will help us to do that.

It is divided into four main sections: Race Relations, the Faith, Community and Evangelism. Inevitably there is a certain amount of overlap, because these things cannot be separated.

To attempt to do evangelism and tell people about the good news of the love and forgiveness of God in Christ has a very hollow ring, and totally lacks conviction, if those who do the telling are failing in their own loving and forgiveness.

There must be good, mutually appreciative relationships between different ethnic groups and people of different colours if a community is to be a good and a healthy one. And, because of our natural tendency to fear people who are different from us, the way for this to change is through faith—and through the perfect love that casts out fear.

The Apostle Paul writes of 'Christ in you, the hope of glory', and says that 'We proclaim him, admonishing and teaching everyone with all wisdom, so that we may present everyone perfect in Christ. To this end I labour, struggling with all his energy, which so powerfully works in me. I want you to know how much I am struggling for you . . .' (Colossians 1:27—2:1, NIV).

There is a struggle going on in our world for justice and for freedom from oppression, and Christians have to be involved in it. This book will give us a far deeper understanding of the struggle, and show us the way ahead.

Shelagh Brown
Commissioning Editor

PREFACE

I was most gratified some years ago when the eleven-year-old son of a friend of mine in Jamaica, after listening to the broadcast of my sermon at a bishop's consecration service, said to his father in great excitement: 'Dad, I listened to the whole sermon and I understood everything the bishop said!'

This was gratifying because the experience of moving from the West Indies to the Britain of the early sixties, the USA civil rights movement and the rise of black consciousness around the world, the impact of black and liberation theology—all combined to compel me towards a radical look at the Christian faith I espoused.

I found it to be a treasure contained in earthenware 'cultural' jars. I made then a conscious decision that my commendation of Christianity must always be such as could be made with integrity to black and white alike; to mud-hut Africans and those in royal palaces; to today's 'slave' and 'free', to oppressed and oppressor. Now for someone who had been brought up to regard preaching as occasions for the display of erudition and familiarity with the heights of English literature, history and achievements and who had spent some five years in theological college acquiring at least a nodding acquaintance with theology, this was quite a challenge! So the young listener's discovery was most welcome.

The sermons and addresses in this book were not delivered with any thought of publication or for any audiences wider than those immediately addressed. But I would like to think that there is a timelessness and universality about their simplicity which may prove helpful to anyone in whose heart the grace of God is at work.

I am indebted to The Revd Shelagh Brown for her generosity and encouragement; to the worshipping communities of St Stephen with St Thomas, Shepherd's Bush; St Laurence, Catford, and those in the Southwark Archdeaconry and the Croydon Episcopal Area, who over the past thirty-two years have been on the receiving end of my out-pourings, and above all to my wife Ina, whose love, loyalty and support, sometimes expressed in frank and critical appraisal, play no mean part in making me what I am! There are many, many others, individual mention of whom would fill a book, whose encouragement, hopes and expectations of me are aptly expressed in the book's title. To them, elevated as I am on their prayers and good wishes, I will be forever grateful.

✠ *Wilfred Croydon*

INTRODUCTION

WILFRED WOOD: A PROFILE

The Reverend Wilfred Wood, JP, man of God and champion of black rights. A profile by Lionel Morrison. Published in SCOPE, the West Indian Life Magazine in August/September 1972.

Black ministers of the cloth are varied and many. Most look with tearful and fervent eyes on the heaven after life, and so futilely console their suffering black flock that heaven with its abundant supply of milk and honey is, after all, within their grasp, but not whilst they are alive.

These black ministers someone once called kitchen-nigger ministers, as they were and still are more of a danger than a help to blacks. But there are the few, and they are growing fortunately, whose religion is mainly trying to find a way for the black man to get some heaven while he is still down here on earth. Rev. Wilfred Wood, as *SCOPE* shows, is one such black minister.

Writing about black personalities is a hazardous occupation these days, especially when they are still alive and can answer back, or as it is more usual, answer behind one's back sideways. On the other hand my Zulu grandma always used to tell me that no black should be mealy-mouthed about other blacks.

Since a black writer is an enquirer, an analyst and purveyor of what happens in the black world, the odds are that he usually smells whether black personalities who are doing things in society for their community, are really trying. That is, whether they are genuine.

With quite a few black personalities, I just cannot help being mealy-mouthed, in spite of my grandma's wise teachings. So that instead of apologizing for them, I try to pay not too much attention to them. My nostrils pick up nothing or rather, they pick up very little.

But Wilfred Wood, JP, man of God and champion of Black rights, is another kettle of fish. He is a man who is genuine, who is really trying, and who definitely commands attention.

In his modest terraced home in London's Shepherd's Bush area, I waited for him. He had just taken his one-year-old son, who had burned himself, to hospital. The sitting room was all disorderly. Kiddie's toys lay scattered on the floor. But in spite of it all I got a feeling of peace prevailing in that house.

The disorderliness in the room was not one that comes about through laziness, but from an understanding that there is more to children's clutter than meets the eye. It was this putting first of human happiness and contentment which I found to be so central to Wilfred Wood.

Born in Barbados in 1936 Wood was educated at Combermere School. He obtained six O levels in the GCE exams and had entered the sixth form and begun to work for his A levels when in 1954 the local government post in St Joseph of Parochial Assessor became vacant.

At the age of eighteen, Wilfred was the youngest of the 29 candidates for the job and his appointment caused some controversy because some people thought he was too young for such a responsible job.

Three years later, when he relinquished the post much to the surprise of many—to enter Codrington College to study for the priesthood—his praises, for ability and integrity, were being sung by one and all, including those who had opposed his appointment.

This decision to enter the ministry was typical of Wood. It was a deliberate act, well thought out and serious. His qualities for leadership were well illustrated at Codrington where he became a central figure. He was always at his best filling posts to which he had been *elected* by his fellow students. He stood up for them, defended them against authority with a passion that was rare at the College.

This involvement in the problems and concern with the troubles of his fellow human beings is in the great tradition of that famous injunction made by Terence, the poet and writer, when he said, '*Homo sum; humani nihil a me alienum puto.*' Which, if my Latin serves me right, simply means: 'I am a man, and anything that concerns mankind involves me.' It was this concern and involvement with anything that concerns mankind, and in this instance his fellow black man, that led him to England.

The late fifties were bad years for racial harmony in this country—not that there has ever been such a thing as racial harmony here. It manifested itself in overt forms, culminating in the Notting Hill 'riots'. 'The official line taken by the British was heard over the BBC in Barbados. We could not understand the way things were being done in Britain, the way life was organized here,' Wood remembered.

'I thought of being a go-between. But I also clearly saw my ministry as not only having to help people to be good, but to be able to tell them how. So I had to see how they lived.' And with that in mind he decided to offer his services for work in England. In 1962 he went to work in Shepherd's Bush, less than a mile from Notting Hill. He remained there for some time.

After a three-year curacy, he was priest-in-charge during an interregnum of seven months before being a senior member of an 11-man group ministry in the area. He has preached on three occasions in the historic Westminster Abbey, in various cathedrals and universities throughout England.

Six years ago (1966) he married a Barbadian girl, Ina, who has been an enormous help to him in his work. They have three children, Gillian, 4, John, 2 and William, 1.

Rev. Wood has done a great deal of work on BBC radio and television. In addition to articles for newspapers and magazines he has made a major contribution to the book *The Committed Church* and is co-author of a hard-hitting anti-racialist book *Vicious Circle*. *The Times* not so long ago devoted the best part of three columns to a description of him and his work, and he has just agreed for a BBC television producer to make a film of his work.

But in spite of all this wooing from the establishment Wilfred Wood has never been bought over. He has not become Uncle Tommish, nor has he compromised his belief that blacks will not be satisfied until, in the words of the prophet Amos, 'justice rolls down like water and righteousness like a mighty stream'.

Just as the Christian maintains his allegiance to the kingdom of God, the black man must also maintain his allegiance to the idea of resistance to racial injustice. Here one is also reminded of the words of that other great black leader Martin Luther King when he said that 'this sweltering summer of the Negro's legitimate discontent will not pass until there is an invigorating autumn of freedom and equality.'

On this question of justice and injustice there can be no compromise, for justice, Wood was taught (like other boys in West Indian schools) had to be equated with truth. British justice on the other hand was a compromise, he found, between two opposing forces. Once justice was compromised it could never be the truth any more.

'I see no contradiction in my active following of Christ and my work to help blacks to greater understanding of their problems and to help them achieve justice.' This justice is not only in the future, a promise, but it must relate to the need of the moment of the black community. Blacks cannot live on promises of justice in the future, he maintains. They must be helped immediately, not as a palliative, a pill to calm them down so that they will not ask for the full works tomorrow, but as a small beginning to complete satisfaction. Christ, after all, did not only speak about the Kingdom to come and the satisfaction that would be the lot of man in future. He looked also to the needs of the moment, as was so aptly shown in his turning water into wine when the wedding hosts ran out of drinks.

Wood thus presents Jesus as a capable, brave, great and lovable man; who is fully related to human life and not a myth that has been changed into a jewel-encrusted painting of an icon.

It is in this light that we must therefore look at Wilfred Wood's active community work among and for blacks. It is a question of Christian reconciliation—the need to stand firmly and uncompromisingly on the side of the black man and articulate the shortcomings of society—shortcomings which British society is not keen to talk and act about.

He wants to see blacks happy, but not the happiness of mere enjoyment, of the lotus eater, but the happiness of the energetic and useful life, which they are denied in this country.

He is chairman and founder of International Personnel—an employment agency dedicated to finding jobs for blacks. Jobs equal to their ability, not merely dead-end jobs. The agency started work about four years ago and in its first year placed ten per cent of all applicants in jobs. For anyone who knows the difficulties blacks have in finding jobs—essentially because of their colour—such an agency's presence cannot be underestimated. It is fighting an uphill battle against industry's racial practices, but Wood sees this as a challenge.

In 1967 Rev. Wood invited to his house five other blacks living in the Shepherd's Bush area, and out of this the Shepherd's Bush Social and Welfare Association was born. It now has its own premises, a former church hall, and provides facilities for a black youth club, steel band, and for wedding receptions and socials.

Above all, there are regular evening classes to help children with their school work. These classes are supervised by a Barbadian, who is a former teacher.

Wood believes that the dignity and the integrity of the black man must be respected as long as the individual does not assault the dignity and integrity of others. Here is an eloquent praise for self-reliance—respect and self-respect for the black man. This idea, in spite of white society's spasm of excitement and fear over political fanaticisms that would fetter and regiment us, is by no means an isolated idea. It is the centre of the black man's revival process, his re-awakening. Wood's vice-presidency of the Martin Luther King Foundation, a charitable organization which helps self-help groups, is in consonance with this basic belief of his.

So is his involvement in the Shepherd's Bush Housing Association, which he helped to found together with The Revd John Ashbridge. Housing, as with employment, is a major problem for blacks in this country. In three years this association had provided decent living conditions for more than ninety families, many of them black.

But his involvement does not end there. In Wood there is a tremendous boiling over of creative energy which leads him still into further avenues where blacks suffer. As one of the founder-members of the HARAMBEE (Swahili for working together in harmony) in Islington, London, he has fully involved himself in the battle between black juveniles and the police, making very clear his concern and championship of black youth.

The project is described as an effort in cooperation between juveniles, parents and police. But in practice it means more than that. It is an attempt to help black youth get proper legal advice—defence, bail etc.—and provide facilities for them to get together and 'do their thing' without the restraints of a hostile society and away from the street haunts.

Wood too is a politician of the highest order—the order of the Holy Ghost. His party is not Labour, Liberal or Tory. His party is the wide, teeming seas of humanity, especially black humanity. It is for this reason that he has never found himself compromised politically, because his constitutency has always been the ordinary black man. He has never been forced to kow tow to the white liberals or the establishment and he has never had to look over his shoulder, as so many black leaders have been forced to do, to see whether he was not displeasing his white masters.

Deliberate, circumspect, serious and shocked almost to the point of being noticeable, Wood seems aloof from the English imagination which is lazy, sociable and heretical and as a rule hostile to intellectual formalization. Many of them cannot understand his pungent criticism of the race relations industry. Criticism which went on even before the existence of the Race Relations Act, which brought into the existence the Community Relations Commission.

He has been intensively critical of the CRC and the unrepresentativeness of most of its black members, who are nominated by the Home Secretary. His criticisms have been echoed and supported by other blacks in this country, who believe that those blacks who serve on the CRC are, rightly or wrongly, 'yes-men' and 'Uncle Toms'. To overcome or meet this criticism Wood put forward what have now become famously known as 'The Wood Proposals', which among other things call for the election by blacks of black members of the CRC. The CRC and the Home Secretary ignored this suggestion, and the CRC has found itself in the invidious position where the majority of blacks—the very people whom the race relations industry is so much dependent upon—reject it and regard it as an establishment body which is here to act as an official buffer to any real expression of black people's rights.

As a member of the board of the British Council of Churches' community relations unit, he was one of the people responsible for drafting the Council's strong condemnation of the recent (1971) Immigration Bill—a statement which was used extensively by the Archbishop of Canterbury in his speech against the Bill.

In an article on the Bill published in *Race Today*, Rev. Wood had this to say:

'The debate about colour in Britain has ended. The impotence of the few who believe that the presence of black people in Britain is a good thing for this country has been so embarrassing that the very ruthlessness with which the Government is carrying out its racist mandate comes as a merciful release. Black people are not wanted in this country; there are too many already; this number must decrease rather than increase...

'Perverse creativity produced the terms "patrial" and "non-patrial". So an East African Asian who fought the Mau Mau to preserve British control of Kenya and was rewarded with British citizenship would be non-patrial, with no right of abode in his country; the South African, Australian or Canadian whose grandfather left this country 150 years ago, and who himself knows England only as the land which produced Len Hutton and Christine Keeler, would nonetheless be patrial with a right of abode...

'Now the next logical step... is to make repatriation compulsory for certain categories of people who are not likely to find champions in this society. I find that the more assurances I get from British officers and gentlemen that repatriation will be voluntary, the more resigned I become to the inevitability of compulsory repatriation...

'There still remains the problems of black people born here. Still, one thing at a time. Hitler did think about repatriating Jews to Guyana or Rhodesia before he hit upon a more complete solution.'

Wood was at the forefront of the struggle to radicalize the Institute of Race Relations, which was dominated by distant big businessmen with little real interest in involving the grassroots. Together with others he succeeded in getting big business ousted—and set about radicalizing the Institute. Today it has more support from the black community, not only in its governing committees but in membership also. It was principally his noticeable presence which enabled it to get a substantial grant from a Foundation to continue its work. Wood was unanimously elected Chairman of the Institute, which is no mean achievement if one recognizes the barbed-wire intricacies of the race relations industry.

In January 1974 he resigned as Chairman of the Institute and was inducted the next month as Vicar of St Laurence, in Catford.

He was very surprised when he was made a Justice of the Peace, which means he sits as a magistrate once a fortnight in the West London Courts.

Wood is a sharp sniper at black armchair leaders, as he is of those pussy-footed white liberals. He recognises that the manhood struggle of the blacks is a very difficult and complicated one. There is nothing especially romantic about it, he reminds one. Yet he is mindful of the trials and suffering blacks have been forced to go through.

Hope, he has. Optimism as well, in awaiting the great day when blacks will be treated like fellow human beings everywhere. The Scripture, I remember, speaks of the great multitudes, coming up from every nation, and Mahalia Jackson, great songster of gospel, sings a song familiar to the ear and spirit: 'These are they,' she sings, 'from every nation on their way to the great coronation, coming up through great tribulations, on their way to the crown in glory.'

Of course there is criticism of Wood. Some of it snobbish; some of it understandable. Some of it tends to degenerate into treating him as a refined form of crossword puzzle. 'I just cannot make him out. He seems too good to be true,' one very well-known white liberal was once heard to remark.

But more to the point was the observation made by a clergyman who had been thrown out of South Africa because of his anti-racialist stand. 'One is attracted to Wood because there is a certain spiritual or intellectual pride and simplicity in his seeking, as a black man, to bear the pain of his time.'

That, I think, is the nearest anyone has ever come to unravelling the Christian simplicity that makes up Wilfred Wood, man of God and champion of Black rights, who, in the vivid phraseology of that great black man, Martin Luther King, 'will not be satisfied until justice rolls down like water and righteousness like a mighty stream'.

Section One

Race Relations

I

SPEECH TO THE GENERAL SYNOD OF THE CHURCH OF ENGLAND

10 November 1988

A few months ago my six-year-old daughter was sitting on my knee in our kitchen. She put her arm around my neck and said, 'Dad, I hope this isn't going to offend you, but I don't want to be in this family any more.' 'Oh!' I said, 'and why don't you want to be in this family any more?' 'Because,' she said, 'I would like to be white and live in a white family.'

I begin with this story not to tug at your heartstrings but to make a point fundamental to our discussion today—namely, that there is a quality about being black in this British society today which can only be expressed and communicated by us black people ourselves. I remember some lines which go like this:

It is easy to sit in your carriage
and counsel the man on foot,
But dismount and walk
and you'll change your talk,
as you feel the nail in your boot!

It is easy to tell the poor man
how he should carry his pack,
But how can you rate
the burden's weight
unless it has been on your back?

It follows, therefore, that in any forum which genuinely seeks meaningful black participation there can be no substitute for the presence of black people.

I use the word *participation* advisedly, and I would draw your attention to the fact that this is the word used throughout this report in preference to 'representation'. Parliament, local government, trade unions, clubs and democratic institutions may order themselves on the basis of *representation* and, therefore, talk of quotas, lobbies, majority votes and so on may rightly be applied to them. But I should have no need to remind this Synod that the Catholic Church of Jesus Christ is like nothing else on earth, or anything else that the world has ever known.

What empire, nation, parliament or borough council has there ever been where the supreme motivation in all things and at all times is meant to be *love*? And what institution is there whose members derive their sense of worth from that claim that 'while we were yet sinners Christ died for us' and they therefore lay claim not to *rights* but to privileges?

My sisters and brothers, we serve the secular world ill if we take our cue from them and so order the life of the Church on the same patterns they have devised in deference to power. We would fail to offer them a model of participation and fellowship made workable by respect and love.

This Synod already recognizes that in certain groups of Christians in this country there is an abundance of wisdom, experience and specialist knowledge which should be made available to Synod. Arrangements are therefore made to ensure the participation of such groups. Women deacons, members of religious communities and service chaplains are among those who occupy seats in this Synod available to no one else. Indeed, my own presence here is a good example of participation rather than representation. Let me explain.

Our Church of England is presently served by a fine body of experienced and gifted men in their capacity as Suffragan Bishops and a limited number of seats are earmarked to secure their participation in the affairs of Synod. Recently, one of these seats became vacant. There are a number of such Suffragan Bishops whose knowledge and experience of Synod and its ways better equip them to *represent* Suffragan Bishops than I could ever do. Indeed, I cast my vote for one such person. But my colleagues judged that it was my participation that they wanted and so, without any manifesto from me outlining how I would represent them, they voted for me. Synod clearly approved of their preference, because the occasion of my introduction to Synod was the closest I have ever come to a near-standing ovation simply for having my name read out!

In setting up the Committee on Black Anglican Concerns, this Synod went to some lengths to ensure black participation. That participation is now reflected in this report because of our special knowledge of the factors which presently inhibit the full measure of black participation in the affairs of the Church of England. I have time to mention only a few of these.

First, even though I have now lived longer in this country than in Barbados where I was born, I am an immigrant from the Caribbean. In the

Caribbean, the vast number of Christians belong to the main-line Anglican, Roman Catholic and Methodist churches, and only a minority to small independent churches, some of which are Pentecostal. But I personally know too many of my Anglican fellow immigrants who can recount their rejection from specific Anglican churches when they first came to this country to underestimate the widespread incidence of this rejection.

Many fell back on reading their Bibles on their own in their rooms as a substitute for public worship, eventually linking up with others in the independent black churches. Some turned their backs on organized religion altogether. The latter could not commend Christianity to their children. The former took their children with them to the black churches. In either case, an entire generation of young black people has been lost to the Church of England.

Secondly, there is a particular feature of black religious experience in which great emphasis is placed on the call from God to any office in the Church. In the Caribbean, Church officers are held in high esteem in the community, so these offices may be coveted for the wrong reasons of personal ambition or status. It is, therefore, considered most unseemly for a person to put himself or herself forward for office, and not likely to be of God. That call is thought to come through the Church leadership, usually the pastor.

A priest-friend of mine in Jamaica tells the story of how he called a church member and said to him, 'I think you have gifts which would be useful in the ministry of the Church.' 'But,' protested the young man, 'I have not been called!' 'Young man,' said the priest, 'what do you think I am doing now?'

So the Church leadership needs to indicate to such black people that they are being called to this kind of service. Our proposals are designed to send that clear message.

At the same time, we know that in centuries of nationhood there are institutions in this country that have managed without the participation of black people. We would be naïve in the extreme if we did not acknowledge that there are those in this country who are determined that this status quo should be maintained. We do not believe this to be true of Synod, but I would ask of those who take issue with our proposals (while at the same time protesting their enthusiasm for black participation) to remind us of the alternative initiatives they have themselves taken in this direction.

For I would repeat here what I have said elsewhere and miss no opportunity of saying. A Britain with black people is a better *Britain* than one without. I look forward to the day when every level of life—Parliament, high court judges, diplomatic service—all reflect the multi-ethnic composition of a country in which there is equality of opportunity, and cultural diversity, in an atmosphere of mutual appreciation. Who better than the Church to be in the forefront of such a movement, and why should Synod not make this tiny contribution?

Thirdly, racism bestrides our society like a colossus.

Report after report by government departments, research bodies and interested groups show black people to be on the receiving end of injustice arising from racial prejudice.

It is so much the everyday experience of so many black people that to protest at every incident could become almost a full-time occupation. For some people an easier means of coping is to minimize the areas of exposure, but this has its drawbacks. I remember some years ago, when black youngsters were being routinely charged with SUS (being a suspected person) that youth leaders were instructing the youngsters that whenever they had occasion to visit the West End they should keep their hands in their pockets at all times. I protested at this on the grounds that once this was established as the norm it would be assumed that any black youngster in the West End who did not have his hands in his pockets was indeed up to no good.

But minimizing areas of exposure to racial prejudice affects your relationship with voluntary associations and, unlike work or school, the Church *is* a voluntary association.

I am aware that our use of the term 'black' has been questioned. For some time now I have made the point when addressing audiences on the subject of race relations to give the audience a choice of terms. I would say that we may either speak of black people and white people, or of 'coloured' people and 'colourless' people. Because black and white are both colours, whereas 'coloured' is not colour, invariably people choose black and white.

The point here is that both groups of people see themselves as normal whereas to use the terms 'white' and 'coloured' is to suggest that anything other than white is a deviation from normality! So I was pleased that in answer to a question from a member on Monday the Secretary General was able to explain that we worked on the principle of self-designation. That is to say, we believe that every person has a right to determine how he or she wants to be designated. Would that this principle had always been observed, because if it had the English language would never have known such terms as 'niggers', 'nig-nogs', 'wogs', 'blackamoors', 'coons', 'chinks' and so on.

It is significant that on our Committee five people could roughly be described as European, five as Asian and five as Afro-European or Afro-Caribbean. It was this group—more representative than most—that chose the term 'black'. We black people get used to others finishing our sentences for us and defining us to their satisfaction. We usually cope with this by saying 'quite, quite', and drifting to the other corner of the room.

Let us be clear what the Committee on Black Anglican Concerns would like. We would like a large number of black candidates to be among those standing for election to the 1990 General Synod. We would like a good number of these to be elected and we shall do all we can, both as a Committee and as individuals, to seek out good candidates, encourage them and give them all the help we can. Such good candidates may be high church or low church, open or shut, middle-of-the-road or kerb crawlers—they may even be Catholic or Evangelical. If we are successful, the proposals we are making now will be irrelevant and unnecessary. And what a joy that would be!

But up to the last Synod elections there were fewer than three black people in a Synod of over 550 members and afterwards there were fewer than eight. So there is the possibility that after the 1990 elections, in spite of all our efforts, there may still be fewer than twenty-four. Should this happen, our proposal is that from among those who had stood for election, the number necessary to make up twenty-four should be added to those elected on the basis of the highest votes polled. Please note that these would be *additional* members, so no one would have been deprived of a place in order to make room for black members. Any talk of quotas is therefore out of place.

I have heard the view expressed that no special provision should be made for black people and they should be elected on their merit. Clearly, to those who take this line, 'merit' is something either bequeathed by the electorate, or infallibly recognized by them! By choosing people who had stood for elections and polled votes, we are choosing people who had this 'merit'—although not enough of it!

Twenty-four is a completely arbitrary number because we do not have sufficiently reliable figures of ethnic groups in the Church of England for a credible statistical basis for calculation. Although the report describes some of our thinking and makes references to estimated numbers of black people in Church and country, in the end we discarded such considerations and plucked a number out of the air. But I was interested to hear the Chairman of the Standing Committee, in his answer to Mrs Clarke's question about ensuring representation of women and those from minority ethnic groups on Synod's boards and committees, say that there were so few people from minority ethnic groups available that they would soon be over-burdened. Twenty-four would certainly be a help in this regard. So my advice to anyone about to propose that the number should be reduced to eighteen is the same as the advice of Punch to those about to marry. Don't!

I think it would be appropriate at this point to draw your attention to the membership of the Committee on Black Anglican Concerns. It is unique among Synod boards and committees in the comparatively high number of black people who serve on it. I myself was an unwilling recruit, and there are representatives of all the major Synod boards. Let me pay tribute to the very high calibre of its membership, both black and white, and to the efficiency and splendid service of staff members, Nigel Barnett and Glynne Goordan-Carter. Others must speak for themselves, but I would assert that if the fellowship, mutual respect and good humour which characterize our Committee are typical of Synod committees in general, then our Church of England's synodical structure has a lot to offer the secular world.

Our Committee has been made aware of legal Counsel's opinion that our proposals would require a Measure in Parliament, and also that he is unable to recommend any method of achieving our objective which would not require such a measure if we are not to fall foul of the Race Relations Act. He does not say that we cannot do what we propose, but that it will need a Measure through Parliament to achieve it. We realize that such proceedings are likely to be drawn out and that such a Measure may not be obtained in time for the 1990 elections. Nevertheless, our view is that by putting forward the proposals and seeking such a Measure, Synod would be sending out such a clear statement that our objectives may be achieved ahead of the Measure. We therefore ask Synod to stick with our proposals.

I have heard of a number of objections to our proposals, some of more weight than others. They do not indicate any absence of good will, but rather the presence of other overriding primary loyalties. To misquote Shakespeare's Brutus, 'Not that I love black people less, but that I love STV [= single transferable vote] more!'

Sadly, we must recognize this dilemma which always confronts a minority. There are seldom, if ever, sufficient people among the majority for whom the best interests of the minority take precedence over every other consideration. Loyalty to property values, or to political parties, or to some other concern must always come first. Indeed, I have even heard the fear expressed that the twenty-four black members would always vote *en bloc*. Quite apart from the fact that this is most unlikely, the spectacle of over 550 members of Synod cowering in fear before the onslaught of this horde of twenty-four could be quite entertaining!

I have also heard it said that it would be patronizing to black people to allot us these twenty-four places. If providing black people with a voice in Synod is patronizing, then I must echo the sentiments of the poor man in *Fiddler on the Roof* when he was told that money was a sickness. 'May I be struck with it,' he said, 'and may I never recover!'

I should mention at this point an unhelpful leading article in one of Mr Rupert Murdoch's newspapers and thank the Bishop of Willesden for his more than adequate response. The article claimed that 'Synod's credibility rests solely on the integrity of the democratic process by which Synod members are elected.' There are some of us who prefer to claim that Synod's credibility rests solely on its faithfulness to the guidance of God's Holy Spirit.

The Church is not a creation of the democratic process. We know whose creation the Church is. If a particular system of election is not enabling the Church to hear God's voice when he chooses to speak through any of his servants, it is the Church's right—even its duty—to adapt and adjust that system in ways that would meet the needs of the Church.

This Synod, I hope, is sensitive to a particular difficulty which faces any body dealing with matters concerning its minorities. Whenever the system that has produced us is called into question it is difficult as individuals not to feel our own place and worth being challenged. After all, a system that has produced *us* cannot be all that bad! So, however much each of us tries to view things impartially, there is therefore an inbuilt imbalance. Now, in the days of slavery when slaves had to be more than careful about saying anything with which their masters might disagree, the slaves used fables as a means of social comment and teaching.

One such fable is of the farmyard dispute between ducks and a goose. The goose was persuaded to take her case to court. When the goose arrived for the hearing, she discovered that the judge was a duck, the jury were all ducks, the prosecuting counsel was a duck and the defending counsel was a duck. Surprise, surprise, she lost the case!

Finally and sadly, I must also tell you that the deliberations of General Synod are not seen by most black people as having the slightest ameliorating effect upon their day-to-day lives. Not even when Synod staged a debate of the highest standard, with speeches well researched and arguments virtually unanswerable, as it did some years ago on the Government's immigration policy, did it manage to temper the harshness of unjust immigration rules. I would be misleading you if I gave the impression that black people would feel better protected from racial harassment, abuse and discrimination if we succeed in getting twenty-four black members onto Synod.

Nor could I be certain of its place in black people's struggle to maintain self-esteem and dignity in the face of disparaging images and racist attitudes.

Nevertheless, I ask you to receive this report.

2

'CORETTA KING SPEAKS'

Address delivered at Central Hall, Westminster, on 17 March 1989, at the public meeting 'Coretta King Speaks'

The life and work of Dr Martin Luther King is of the greatest significance to this country because it is of the greatest significance to the world. It would be presumptuous to suggest that any one facet of his work was more important than any other, but we in this country owe him a special debt on two counts.

First, when he drew international attention to the plight of black people in America, we in this country could no longer refuse to see our own reflection in the mirror he was holding up, and today we recognize that the black minority in this country is also on the receiving end of the injustice which results from bigotry and racialism.

Secondly, his work showed that the mere juxtaposition of injustice and good intentions does not result in improvement—action is necessary, and an essential part of this action is the legitimate demand for justice from those who suffer.

From time to time I am invited to speak on the immigrants' contribution to this country—remembering that the word 'immigrant' is a polite form of reference to black people—and dutifully I repeat that in the Health Service nearly 50 per cent of all junior staff (doctors below the status of consultant) are immigrants; that the mental hospitals, the district hospitals and the geriatric wards of large hospitals rely heavily on immigrant nursing staff; that the building industry, public transport and other public services could possibly grind to a halt if all immigrant labour was withdrawn.

But I would be doing both the black and white sections of our community the greatest disservice if I paraded these facts as the ground on which black people's claim for civilized treatment and the right to live peaceably in this country was based. It would be a disservice because it might suggest that the status of being human is to be earned by being useful, and in this way make communication even more difficult between those who have never doubted that they are human, and those who require proof that this is so.

But because it is fashionable to equate colour prejudice with patriotism, and because the presence of black people in this country is represented as a threat to the fine British heritage passed down to the present generation of Englishmen and which must be passed on to future generations, I feel I must refer you to some words spoken by Sir Winston Churchill just before the Second World War:

The West Indies, two hundred years ago, bulked very largely in the minds of all people who were making Britain and the British Empire. Our possession of the West Indies, like that of India—the colonial plantation and development as they were then called—gave us the strength, but especially the capital, the wealth at a time when no European nation possessed such a reserve, which enabled us, not only to acquire this world-wide appendage of possessions which we have, but also to lay the foundations of that commercial and financial leadership, which, when the world was young, when everything outside Europe was undeveloped, enabled us to make our great position in the world.

I have no reason to doubt the truth of Sir Winston's statement, and the statement shows that the so-called immigrants are no less entitled to the benefits of living in this comparatively affluent society than are those who now enjoy unearned incomes from wealth amassed by others many years ago.

The task to which we must apply ourselves is that of ensuring that this country thrives, not in spite of its black minority, but because of it. That there is the minimum wastage of the ability, zeal and drive which is to be found in minority communities. It is not enough that here and there a black superman should win recognition because he *is* a superman, or that a necessary condition for his advancement should be that he is unlike other black people. It is not enough that minority communities should be asked to identify with a few specially selected tokens. The avenues for movement in the spheres of industry, politics and public service must be so free of racial barriers that the black person's only requirement for success should be integrity, ability and self-respect. If this is so, and is seen to be so, then this country is only on the threshold of the greatness that can be hers.

So it is important that we who are working for the ideal of a fully integrated, multi-racial society in this country should recognize a new factor which has entered the situation as a result of two events in recent months. The first was the panic which stampeded the government into passing the Commonwealth Immigrants Act, and the second was the eruption of racism following two notorious and emotive speeches. This new factor is that no agency—official or otherwise—even those working for harmonious race relations in this country, can demand or expect the unqualified trust of immigrant communities. How are immigrants to know that other well-timed and well-publicized assaults on their right to share in the life of this country will not result in further panic and even further restrictions? Surely a demand that no more immigrants should be allowed in Wolverhampton must imply the carrying of pass-books by immigrants to show that they belong to Wolverhampton! And if workers in a factory can go on an anti-immigrant strike and be complimented on their action by the management, can anyone blame the immigrant who finds normal industrial relations machinery somewhat suspect?

It seems to me that the liberal elements in our society must be prepared to work alongside immigrant communities without automatically enjoying their confidence, and certainly without presuming to have a right to it. We must expect to be judged by our deeds rather than by our words, and the help we offer must not be on condition that *we* provide the leadership, that we dictate the tactics, that we be assured at all times of unswerving loyalty, because this would be to make no contribution to the security and self-respect of the immigrant communities which in the long run will be the most stabilizing factor in race relations in this country.

No: the immigrants' contribution does not lie in cheerfully providing labour to keep essential services going until such time as they can be modernized and improved by automation. It lies in sharing the same ambitions and achievements of a good citizen of a good country. If, in the years to come, he is able to do this whatever may be the colour of his skin or the birthplace of his grandfather, then it will be because England has become a country in which there is equal opportunity with cultural diversity and mutual tolerance. He would then have made his contribution to the finest country in the world!

The Martin Luther King Foundation can make some contribution to this goal, and we are fortunate that we are being honoured by the presence of Mrs Coretta King on this occasion of its launching. If we all recognize the abundant virtues of the man after whom the Foundation takes its name—and if we earnestly desire to continue the work he began, then we will not need to be reminded that Dr King would not have wanted us to vaunt his uniqueness. He would have pointed us to the many things he had in common with the people in the street we never glance at twice—a bus conductor here, a railway porter there. When such people come to live next door to us and we immediately sell our property and flee to an all-white neighbourhood it may be another Martin Luther King we are despising. What price then, our lip-service to his memory?

'Then the righteous will answer him, "Lord, when did we see you...?" The King will reply, "I tell you the truth, whatever you did for one of the least of these brothers of mine, you did for me."

'Then he will say to those on his left, "Depart from me . . ." They also will answer, "Lord, when did we see you . . .?" He will reply, "I tell you the truth, whatever you did not do for one of the least of these, you did not do for me." '

Matthew 25:37–45 (NIV)

3

THE GOOD NEIGHBOUR

Sermon preached in Westminster Abbey, Sunday 25 October 1983

A teacher of the Law came up and tried to trap Jesus. 'Teacher,' he asked, 'what must I do to receive eternal life?'

Jesus answered him, 'What do the Scriptures say? How do you interpret them?'

The man answered, ' "Love the Lord your God with all your heart, with all your soul, with all your strength, and with all your mind"; and "Love your neighbour as you love yourself." '

'You are right,' Jesus replied; 'do this and you will live.'

But the teacher of the Law wanted to justify himself, so he asked Jesus, 'Who is my neighbour?'

Jesus answered, 'There was once a man who was going down

from Jerusalem to Jericho when robbers attacked him, stripped him, and beat him up, leaving him half dead. It so happened that a priest was going down that road; but when he saw the man he walked on by, on the other side. In the same way a Levite also came along, went over and looked at the man, and then walked on by, on the other side. But a Samaritan who was travelling that way came upon the man, and when he saw him, his heart was filled with pity. He went over to him, poured oil and wine on his wounds and bandaged them; then he put the man on his own animal and took him to an inn, where he took care of him. The next day he took out two silver coins and gave them to the innkeeper. "Take care of him," he told the innkeeper, "and when I come back this way, I will pay you whatever else you spend on him." '

And Jesus concluded, 'In your opinion, which one of these three acted like a neighbour towards the man attacked by the robbers?'

The teacher of the Law answered, 'The one who was kind to him.'

Jesus replied, 'You go, then, and do the same.'

Luke 10:25–37 (GNB)

If I were to name as the subject of our meditation this morning the parable of the good *neighbour*, the chances are that you might be uncertain about which of Our Lord's parables I have in mind. On the other hand, should I make reference to the parable of the good *Samaritan*, you would recognize immediately the reference to the parable we have just heard read. The interesting thing is that Our Lord told this story in answer to the question, 'Who is my *neighbour*?'—and the answer surely is that the neighbour is anyone who acts with compassion towards a fellow human being. That would still have been the complete answer had Our Lord merely said that 'a third man' who came by helped the distressed traveller.

As it happens, Our Lord said that the third man was a Samaritan. But why is it that we today prefer to name this story, not 'the parable of the good *neighbour*', or even 'the parable of the *Samaritan* neighbour', but instead 'the parable of the *good* Samaritan?' Let us hazard a guess.

When the Hebrew people lived in slavery in Egypt, they did not divide themselves into Jews and Samaritans. They all knew a common oppression, and they all came to recognize the one true God who broke their chains, and set them free to love and serve him, first in their wanderings in the wilderness, and later in peace and prosperity in Palestine. Unfortunately, King Rehoboam surrounded himself with 'yes-men', lost touch with the common people, and soon had a civil war on his hands. The people of the north broke away and established Samaria as their capital city, and became a prosperous commercial people known as Samaritans. The people of the south retained Jerusalem as their capital and came to be known as Jews.

But the more the Samaritans outdid the Jews in prosperity, the more the Jews prided themselves on their own *so-called* pure lineage and ancestry, and derided the northerners as a polyglot nation. So by the time of Our Lord, a Samaritan was, in the eyes of the Jews, the lowest form of life on earth. A Samaritan was a nothing, a nobody, not because of anything he did, but because of what he was—he was from a race that was at the bottom of the pile, and for the Jews that would always be the most important fact about him.

When Our Lord told this parable, and named the good neighbour as a Samaritan, there was only one way in which his Jewish hearers could accept the obvious point and yet keep their anti-Samaritan prejudices undisturbed. They could say, 'Ah, but he was not typical—he was different. He was a *good* Samaritan!'

My own sad conclusion is that today we too prefer the title 'the good Samaritan' rather than the good neighbour because our own thinking is so much like theirs. We too think and act on the basis of racial stereotypes, and not even superhuman feats of *individuals* in the fields of learning, craftsmanship, invention or sport will disturb our deep-seated prejudices. Such individuals are the exceptions which prove the rule, we say.

If proof were needed to support this claim, we need only to point to the position of black people in Britain today. Alongside the distinctive achievements of some black individuals, there is the daily experience of petty acts of racial discrimination which is the lot of most black people; the constant reminders that by your colour you are a member of a group of undesirables. You do not have to be a black member of a group of friends on a day-trip to France, who with other black persons are denied admission and must remain at the quayside until your white friends return in the evening. You cannot avoid going into shops, even though you know that you must make your selections with the store detective making no effort to conceal his interest in you, and his close attention to your every move. To be the teenage son of thrifty black parents who buy a house away from Brixton means being stopped by policemen and challenged to prove that you live where you say you live—to quote the telephone number, produce your house-key and so on.

Two weeks ago a fellow-priest from Barbados learned the hard way not to be alone on an Underground station platform at 11 o'clock on a Saturday night—when he regained consciousness in St Bartholomew's Hospital the next day, following the attentions of a gang of hooligans.

Two weeks ago the national press reported that the government is going ahead with plans to divide people who claim unemployment benefit into racial groups. Staff at benefit offices will be asked to assess claimants visually and categorize them as West Indian, African, Asian, etc. Why is it so important that there should be recorded the colour of a man's skin when he claims the financial assistance to which unemployed people are entitled? Is it to provide some semblance of respectability to those who claim that black people are a drain on the economy of this country? Already I can hear certain members of Parliament claiming that black unemployed people cost the country so many thousands of pounds and how much cheaper it would be to grant-aid them to leave the country.

So far as I know there has been no outcry or outrage against this blatant racism. *The truth is that this kind of behaviour on the part of both Government and individuals is possible only because there is a virus of racism in our national life; that it is actively fostered by some people for their own ends, and is no longer a matter of concern or shame for the majority.*

By choosing a Samaritan, a member of a despised race, to be the benefactor in this story, Our Lord showed that neighbourliness is something which cuts across all barriers, racial and political differences, and even personal likes and dislikes. He shows that to do service to others in need is indeed neighbourly conduct, so the rich should help the poor, the strong should help the weak and so on. But he shows something else. He knew that such acts have in them the seeds of patronage and condescension, and this could lead to complacency and pride.

So this story has another lesson—the lesson of humility. There will be times when the neighbour will be someone from whom you will want to receive no favours, and to whom you will not want to be indebted. There are many people who enjoy being generous to others, but will accept no favours from them, forgetting that the other person's kindness and generosity are as important to his or her self-fulfilment as their own is to them.

This is a lesson which the Church accepts in theory but is reluctant to put into practice. True, we no longer hold crude theories about humanity being divided into 'superior races' and 'lesser breeds', or that Europe is made up of 'nations' while Africa is made up of 'tribes'. But we still have a long way to go. We still have to recognize that it may please God to speak to us through the Samaritans of today's world—those whom we consider to be the despised or the inferior—and that we need to be humble enough to recognize and accept this.

I am continually being reminded of an episode in a book written almost twenty-five years ago entitled *The Lonely African*. The writer recalls how he was standing with a white farmer observing an African worker. The African wore only a pair of shorts, but around his neck was a tie! (probably a regimental tie!) The farmer commented that the silly fellow did not realize that one did not wear a tie without a shirt and collar! His more observant companion had already noted that for the African the tie was not a piece of clothing but had become a useful piece of equipment. He used it to tie bundles of wood, and it was only when it was not in use that he kept it around his neck!

Because the European so often looks at Africa through spectacles clouded by notions of racial superiority, he sees only the African's clumsy handling of European concepts and commodities, and has no perception of the African's ingenuous adaptation of a new thread to be woven into the strong and authentic tapestry which has stood the test of time.

So it is with black people's experience of God. It is true that in Africa, the Caribbean and elsewhere there may be found church buildings modelled on ancient cathedrals in this country, and choirs robed in cassocks and Canterbury caps struggling with Anglican chants. It is true that there are records of priests going out from this country to minister to large black congregations overseas. But it is worth remembering that, even while theologians were debating whether or not black people had souls and were fit subjects for baptism, black people, by their experience of pain, of life and death in all its starkness, in the companionship which is bred in a common oppression, had laid hold upon the God unto whom all hearts are open, all desires known; the God who could, and would, exalt the valleys, and make plains of the mountains—the God who held them always in the hollow of his hand.

It was an easy mistake for the European to believe that they were receiving God at *his* hands—and for the first time—when they were allowed into the galleries of the churches, and therefore to assume that their religion was only a reflection of his. Now, Europe having pronounced God dead, or at any rate mummified in a religion which has no power to change the lives of men and women, it would not occur to them to look to the black presence in their midst for the authentic word of God today.

Yet the marks of true religion are to be found in Britain's black communities. *Suffering* there certainly is, but there is also *faith*. There is *hope* and, above all, there is *love*. There is *joy*, and although the rejection of sin and evil sometimes appears theatrical or sanctimonious, for *people*—including sinners—there is always *acceptance*. Moreover, there is a strong sense of the *indivisibility of truth*. Lies are always lies, and must necessarily lead away from God who is Truth. Even white lies are lies! There is a strong sense of *the place of weak persons*, as of right, in the life of the community, whether they be elderly people or small children. *Dependence upon God* is seen as strength and not as weakness, and *obedience to God's will* is a virtue, not something to be ashamed of. Where, for others *to speak loudly to Jesus* as to a companion walking alongside might appear a form of mental illness, for a black Christian, conscious of the abiding presence of a living Christ, it is a perfectly reasonable thing to do.

For black Christians who are rooted in the life of the black community the existence of God is not dependent upon the latest utterances of Cambridge theologians, and we can hear the word of God in holy Scripture with or without the aid of form criticism. So, in response to God's call, and with his help, we are determined, with a quiet confidence, that we shall always be good neighbours—Samaritans or not!

4

SLAVES' EMANCIPATION

Sermon preached in St Margaret's, Westminster at a service commemorating the 150th anniversary of the emancipation of slaves, on 17 July 1984

Almost two thousand years ago there was a small subject-nation in the Middle East. A village woman living in this colonial territory had a son who grew up to become a wandering preacher. He had no formal education, and he used illustrations from the life of the people to share his thoughts with anyone who would listen. Although he attracted curiosity and sufficient hostility from the influential people of his time for them to frame him and have him hanged, by far his most profound effect was upon the poorest, most despised and outcast human beings that were around. In his day these were mainly lepers, beggars, handicapped people and prostitutes.

But his effect upon such people was electric. *He changed their thinking about themselves*, and for the first time they saw that the contrived system of social values which was dominant in their day, and by which they were relegated to the scrapheap, was artificial and transitory. The truth was that they were of equal worth with those who despised them and lorded it over them.

Today, all these years later, we recognize that village preacher, Jesus of Nazareth, to be God's full and definitive Word to all humankind, and we see that the perception which came to those outcasts is a truth for all of us. We recognize this Jesus to be *Christ*, that is, the One appointed by God for the ushering in of his kingdom, and we, as baptized Christians, are committed to making this kingdom of God more recognizably a reality. Whenever a Christian prays, that is the purpose of his or her prayer—'Thy will be done on earth as it is in heaven.'

In God's will, neither in heaven nor on earth are there to be slaves and free men. And if that is the purpose of the Christian's *prayer*, it should be no less the purpose of his *work*.

This is true for every Christian whatever job or employment he or she is engaged in. But in a society where the God-given rights of men and women can be either recognized, or denied, by the laws of the land, there are special responsibilities and opportunities for those who share in the making of these laws.

Today we are giving thanks for the faithful way in which a small group of Christians, who were involved in the making of the laws of this land, discharged their responsibilities towards the fulfilment of God's will for the world. The implementation on 1 August 1834 of the Bill to abolish slavery in the British Empire was largely the result of Christian conviction which issued in the effective parliamentary action spearheaded by such people as Wilberforce, Buxton, Sharp, Clarkson, Babington, Grant, Thornton, Macaulay, Stephen, Venn, Gisborne, Teignmouth and Smith.

The work of these parliamentarians has proved to be of the highest significance to the world. These were men who acted not merely because of pressure but on the basis of principle. Up to then it had not been unknown for parliamentarians to stand up for the interests of their class or for their kith and kin. But this was a new development. Here was a case where the evil they sought to abolish was not daily before the eyes of the public to shame them or inconvenience them. Here there were no votes to be gained by championing this cause: no reward of ministerial posts because of service to the government in power.

On the contrary, the black slaves who were to benefit from their efforts had no votes to show their gratitude; the slave owners who would lose property had no goodwill for them, and the government had no love for these troublesome backbenchers whose zeal repeatedly upset and embarrassed them. Today we honour their memory and thank God for their labours.

It is customary these days, in the process of erecting an important building, to mark progress by celebrating at three stages of development. First, there is the breaking of the sod. Next there is the laying of the foundation stone. And finally comes the great day when the commemorative plaque is unveiled to put the seal on all the planning, labour, disappointments and satisfactions that have gone before. I see the achievement of the Clapham Sect, great though it was, to be but the breaking of the sod and the laying of the foundation stone for a certain kind of society.

The odious practice of slavery and the slave trade was allowed to flourish because enough European people basically held the view that black people, because of their blackness, were either sub-human or, at best, an inferior species of humanity. In this country the legislation of 1807 and 1833 dismantled the legal framework of these crude views, but it made only the slightest impression upon the racist attitudes of Europeans. The records of some white colonial régimes in their dealings with the black populations of the colonies were not far removed from the earlier days of slavery, and there are enough recorded utterances of European academics, churchmen and politicians to show that not only ordinary Europeans, but their leaders in thought and national life, continued to see black people as inferior.

Today, in 1984, a white racist régime in South Africa continues to oppress the sons and daughters of God on the basis of the colour of their skin. In that country, a man's blackness, which is part of his personhood, a gift from God in which he should rejoice, is instead the reason for his oppression. He can have no say in the choice of people to make laws to govern him, who can only be white. Within the country in which he is born he is unable to move freely in search of work to support his family.

Those who would speak for him have their passports confiscated—like Bishop Desmond Tutu. Or are made into non-persons by being banned or imprisoned—like Nelson Mandela. Or are shamelessly murdered—like Steve Biko. Meanwhile, representatives of that brutal régime are made welcome by heads of governments in European countries, and not a few members of Parliament in this country are tireless in their efforts to secure for this régime a certificate of respectability.

Nor can we be complacent about the situation in this country. Although the euphemistic terms of 'immigrants' and 'immigration' are used, black people in this country know that the so-called immigration restrictions of 1962, 1965, 1968 and 1971 and the more recent Immigration and

Nationality Act are a concession to the racialism in this country which sees black people as a problem, and a problem which can be managed or eliminated by strict limits upon the numbers of black people in this country. Nor was the recent survey by the Policies Studies Institute telling us anything new when it revealed that 'violent racially motivated attacks on black people are a common and frightening aspect of racialism in Britain'.

Those 'patriotic' football fans from this country who travel abroad to support the English team, and who shout racist abuse whenever a black *English* player touches the ball, know that they have their more sophisticated counterparts in many spheres of life in this country. The Abolitionist parliamentarians may have laid the foundation stone 150 years ago, but the building is by no means complete.

There is a most revealing incident recorded in the tenth chapter of St Mark's Gospel. On one occasion Jesus and his disciples were on their way to Jerusalem for the Passover festival. As they passed through a village they attracted the usual notice and attention as people lined the route to wish the pilgrims God-speed. A blind beggar asked what was going on, and when he heard that it was Jesus he called out to him. The people around him told the beggar to be quiet, but Jesus stopped and said, 'Call him.' When Jesus asked what he wanted, he replied: 'Sir, I want my sight back.' Jesus restored his sight.

I find this incident immensely reassuring on three counts. First of all, above all that noise and clamour, and among people who were able to put themselves forward, Jesus was able to hear the voice of the poor man who needed help. Christ always hears the cry of the oppressed.

Secondly, those who surrounded Jesus advised the blind man to be quiet—it was not the right time or place. But Jesus overruled them. 'Call him', he said.

Thirdly, the poor man wanted no more than what everyone else took for granted—to be able to see.

I am convinced that the struggle for justice on the part of the poor and oppressed people of the world will, in the end, be vindicated. But far too many people who should be in a position to help prefer instead to argue that the time is not ripe, or that demands are ill-timed. But as Martin Luther King wrote in his famous letter from Birmingham jail: 'We must come to see that justice too long delayed is justice denied.'

The poor and the oppressed people must not be discouraged from seeking help or making demands. It is not enough for present-day parliamentarians to glory in the achievements of their honourable predecessors.

Woe to those who make unjust laws, to those who issue oppressive decrees, to deprive the poor of their rights and withhold justice from the oppressed of my people...

Isaiah 10:1–2 (NIV)

Is not this the kind of fasting I have chosen: to loose the chains of injustice and untie the cords of the yoke, to set the oppressed free and break every yoke? Is it not to share your food with the hungry and to provide the poor wanderer with shelter—when you see the naked, to clothe him, and not to turn away from your own flesh and blood? Then your light will break forth like the dawn, and your healing will quickly appear; then your righteousness will go before you, and the glory of the Lord will be your rear guard. Then you will call, and the Lord will answer; you will cry for help, and he will say: Here am I.

If you do away with the yoke of oppression, with the pointing finger and malicious talk, and if you spend yourselves on behalf of the hungry and satisfy the needs of the oppressed, then your light will rise in the darkness, and your night will become like the noonday. The Lord will guide you always; he will satisfy your needs in a sun-scorched land and will strengthen your frame. You will be like a well-watered garden, like a spring whose waters never fail.

Isaiah 58:6–11

The issue of racial justice in Britain today cries out for leadership from those parliamentarians who are not prepared to twist and turn and make corkscrews of themselves in the pursuit of government office or popular acclaim. There are enough people in Parliament who wear the label of 'Christian' who could be worthy successors of Wilberforce, Clarkson, Sharp and Buxton.

The cause is the cause of the powerless. The call is the call from God. All that is needed are conviction and courage—and these can be acquired on the way. It is time to get on with the building of the just, participatory, multi-racial society for which the sod was broken by those Christians in politics known as the Clapham Sect, and whose monument is to be seen wherever black and white people meet in the equal sonship of the One God and Father of all.

5

NEW CROSS FIRE PROTEST MARCH

From an address to the marchers in Fordham Park at the start of the protest march on 2 March 1981 for the fire on 18 January 1981

Today is not a day for speeches. Today is a day for action. And what we are doing today on this demonstration is first and foremost an act of witness. We are witnesses on two grounds.

First, it is a fact that thirteen young people died when Mrs Ruddock's house was maliciously set on fire. It is a fact that all thirteen young people were black. It is a fact that in the past people have been murdered in this country for no other reason than that they were black. It is a fact that so far no culprit has been apprehended and no one charged with the murder of these thirteen people.

We believe that the mothers and fathers of these children, the young widow and her unborn child, are entitled to an explanation. This act of witness is an act of solidarity with the bereaved, and a joining of our thousands of voices to theirs to demand an explanation.

Secondly, we know that views have been expressed in many quarters, including the press and parliament, that 'the solution to race relations in this country is when the indigenous people see that the black population is declining rather than increasing.'

Now, whatever racists many think, God made us black people as we are, to be as we are, and we are not going to commit mass suicide, or withdraw to some overseas reservations simply to indulge those who want an all-white Britain.

So the second reason for this act of witness is to proclaim to all and sundry, to friend and foe alike, to people in this country, to Third World countries, to the United Nations, and to anyone who will listen, that *the black community in Britain is here to stay.*

We want to live in peace and brotherhood with everyone—irrespective of their race, colour or creed. But, in the words of Martin Luther King, 'Either we live together as brothers, or we perish together as fools.'

In either case, the important word is 'together'.

6

RACISM AWARENESS GROUP STUDY

Notes on racism awareness training for a discussion on 2 December 1992 by the Committee on Black Anglican Concerns

This paper should be discussed in small groups, paragraph by paragraph, and agreement or disagreement with each paragraph should be established before moving on to the next.

1. Human beings are by nature self-centred. This leads to high appreciation of self, and at that stage of development when we are most impressionable, infancy and childhood, appreciation of those nearest to us, such as mother and members of our immediate family circle.

2. It is easy to pass from thinking highly of ourselves to thinking little of other people. The less people are 'like us' the more likely we are to think less of them.

3. Ethnic differences, because of their visibility and permanence, provide an easy means of classification as human self-centredness is translated into 'racial' distancing. Thus, individual self-importance and rejection of others solidify into a group norm.

4. This distancing can foster various attitudes depending on social conditioning; attitudes such as reverence, pity, fear, envy, contempt, hatred, admiration, respect and so on.

5. Racism Awareness helps us to identify this process (paragraph 4) at work in our own lives and in the life of whatever ethnic group to which we belong. We are then better placed to devise aids to counteract this process and free us to relate to others as individuals and groups on the basis of their 'true' worth, that is, as equally unique creatures of a God of love who loves and values us equally. 'True' because it is a worth which can neither be enhanced nor diminished by circumstances of birth, nationality, achievement, gender, colour and so on.

6. Racism Awareness Education and Racism Awareness Training are attempts to reduce or reverse this natural bent and to minimize its adverse effects. There is a distinction to be made between Racism Awareness *Education* and Racism Awareness *Training*. Just as in our formal education system a minority of pupils are 'educated', in that their inherent gifts are drawn out and enabled to develop, but a majority are 'trained', so that they are conditioned to respond in a particular way to certain recognizable signals, be it accents, or bearing or manner of dress, Racism Awareness *Education* should come more easily for a Christian, but society would benefit hugely if all and sundry were 'trained'.

7. Racism Awareness Education and Racism Awareness Training will be shaped by context and location. The context of a black South African native and a white European immigrant in South Africa is not the same as that of the white East Londoner in Britain and the immigrant Pakistani here. The contexts of the Asian, the child of white European parents, and the Anglo-Indian, all three born and living in India, vary, as do the contexts of the African, Chinese, Japanese, Korean, Indian, Caribbean, who are all immigrants in Canada.

8. The context for Racism Awareness Education and Racism Awareness Training in Britain is heavily shaded by five considerations:

8.1. While there are numerous ethnic groups in British society, perhaps too many to enumerate, it is skin colour that is the generally accepted broadbrush differentiation.

8.2. Britain's imperialist past and its lucrative involvement in the slave trade and in Europe's cultural and financial pillage of Africa and Asia seep into present-day encounters between on the one hand those whose roots go back to colonized countries, and on the other hand those who are clothed in the comforting memory that Britain won World War Two. In other words, a sense of grievance encountering a sense of pride tinged with arrogance.

8.3. The cult of 'home, sweet home', of perfect contentment consisting of 'security in your own home, in your own neighbourhood, in your own country', makes the immigrant a supplicant, and thus by definition incomplete, and the native his or her superior. This is heightened by the desperate attempts of would-be escapees from the deprivation of the

Southern Hemisphere countries to enter and settle in this country. A demand for equality thus becomes a discordant challenge to the fitness of things.

8.4. A world order in which the decision makers, the rich and the powerful, are invariably 'white' and the Third World of no consequence is presented to us daily in news bulletins, drama and documentaries by television, radio and newspapers.

8.5. We are still very close to the time when a dark skin accurately identified a foreigner, when Britain could be regarded as a 'white' country. Attitudes formed in that era contaminate our perception of native English, Scottish, Welsh and Irish people who happen to be black.

9. In a sense, Racism Awareness Education is not unlike the teaching ministry of Jesus. He pointed to the kingdom of heaven as his 'reality', and in doing so showed up the undesirable characteristics of his hearers' own reality. He invited his hearers to step out of their reality into his. Racism Awareness Education seeks to help people to defy the evidence of their eyes and ears, in which black and white are not equal; in which society's awards and punishments are based less on merit than on ethnicity, and instead, to live *now* in a reality where these things are not so.

10. Successful Racism Awareness Education must necessarily lead to a dissatisfaction with Britain as it is now. It would be characterized not by a resignation to change, but by a desire, even an impatience, for it. Change into the kind of society where black and Asian people may not only be among the prison population, but may also be members of the royal family; where the Tory MP for Cheltenham may be black, to no one's surprise, and, in a Tory Government, be the Foreign Secretary; where the three Lords of Appeal just happen to be of African, Asian and European descent. Racism Awareness Education and training will increase the individual's desire for change and may necessitate painful adjustment of his or her personal circumstances.

11. In the absence of Racism Awareness Education, Racism Awareness Training is necessary for all those who make decisions affecting the life-chances of citizens and potential citizens of this country. The law-abiding citizen has surrendered his 'right' to procure what he needs by 'any means possible' in exchange for protection of the law, and the law's assistance to

live as God intends—i.e. in love and peace with all—she/he will be the loser in this contract if those with the power to do so treat her/him less favourably than others because of ethnic origin, whether they do so consciously or unconsciously. Therefore those with such power should be trained to follow procedures which do not depend upon their personal taste.

12. Racism Awareness Training would be based on the premise that Britain is irrevocably a multi-ethnic, multi-cultural society.

12.1. With this premise, all places of education and learning, from primary school, through university, to adult education institutions, should make provision for all students to engage with this aspect of living by means appropriate to the particular institution.

12.2. Wherever there are criteria for selection for employment, such criteria should require the successful applicant to discharge her/his duties within the spirit of a truly multi-ethnic, multi-cultural enterprise. She/he should be able to demonstrate previous efforts to prepare herself/himself in this way.

12.3. Companies, institutions and public service departments should recognize the need to monitor their own compliance with the spirit as well as the letter of Race Relations legislation, with personnel in their employ afforded leave for appropriate training, refresher courses and so on in Equal Opportunities provision. In awarding contracts, central and local government as well as companies dealing with sub-contractors should insist on demonstrable compliance with Equal Opportunities practice. Whatever 'instrument of control' of the day-to-day management of such enterprises there is (board, council, committee, or executive group) should require from heads of departments regular reports on the implementation of a publicly-known policy.

13. Racism Awareness Education and Racism Awareness Training programmes devised for overtly Christian individuals, agencies and institutions must necessarily differ from those for other social groups, although the end must be the same. The Christian rationale can include the doctrine of creation, that there is one human race which was created by the One Almighty, universal God; of salvation for all through the life, death and resurrection of Jesus; the biblical vision of life in glory with persons

drawn from every nationality and ethnic group and, above all, of grace. Its mode could draw upon life in the body of Christ where sins past and present are confessed and forgiven; where the common dependence upon the mercy of God facilitates reconciliation and mutual respect, and where the gift of the same Holy Spirit changes the aspiration to a life of fellowship, peace and joy into a reality.

14. A Christian-based Racism Awareness Training Unit should be identified by the Church of England and placed at the service of the dioceses. This unit should devise a five-year rolling programme to which all bishops, archdeacons, members of bishops' staff meetings, diocesan heads of departments, and principals and teaching staff of theological colleges and courses should be exposed. It would be hoped that such would be the demand for such training that diocesan boards and committees, schools, bishop's councils, deanery synods, PCCs and parish groups would avail themselves of the services of the unit.

7

TO OVERCOME IS TO UNDERTAKE

Martin Luther King Memorial Lecture, 4 April 1989

Introduction

There is now an annual public holiday in the USA in honour of Dr Martin Luther King—usually on the Monday nearest to his birthday, 15 January. It is most appropriate that America should so honour one of its greatest sons. But King's struggle against injustice in the USA was but a particularity of the worldwide struggle against injustice, wherever it is found, so there is a sense in which his contribution should be appropriately recognized not only in America but in every country which honours the ideals of justice, peace and fellowship for the human race, irrespective of colour, class, creed, ethnic group or gender.

Would that we could be confident that there will soon be a Martin Luther King public holiday in *this* country. But until that day comes it behoves those of us who share King's ideals and honour his memory to express in our own humble and modest way our appreciation of his contribution.

Never tire of telling the story

Recently, I said to one of my younger colleagues, 'Can you remember where you were on the day when the news of Martin Luther King's assassination came through?' 'Yes,' he replied, 'in my pram!' It was a salutary reminder that there are those who recognize King's legacy to be theirs, who share our admiration for, and appreciation of this great man, but who did not hear or see him in his lifetime. They are therefore dependent upon the written record, the spoken word and the film clip.

So we older ones should never tire of telling the story, of reciting the facts and figures, the sayings, the setbacks and the achievements of the people who, at a certain time in history, stood up and walked, and found the courage to do so, because Martin Luther King continually reminded them that their cause was a righteous cause; that God is righteous; that God keeps faith; that they should keep their faces towards God's promised land of freedom, dignity and peace, and stride towards that land with arms linked and with a strong resolve: 'We shall overcome.' So, for the sake of our young people, the story must be told and retold.

There is another reason why we must tell the story. It is simply this. If *we* do not tell it, no one else will. Last year while in the USA I visited the Lincoln Memorial where Martin Luther King made his great 'I have a dream' speech to millions in 1963. I went into the bookshop to buy some cards and while I was there a white woman complained to the sales assistant, 'I thought this was supposed to be the *Lincoln* Memorial. Why are there so many cards and books about Martin Luther King?' The irony of this was that the sales assistant was a black girl!

Tony Brown, the great black American educator, never tires of pointing out that recorded history is selective; that certain people decide what in *their* view is worth recording and what can be forgotten. He would say to his audiences, 'I will ask you three American history questions:

'Number 1. Name three Afro-American heroes of the American War of Independence.

'Number 2. What black American invented the electric traffic lights system?

'Number 3. Who chopped down a cherry tree and could not tell a lie?

'If the last answer is the only one you can answer, the chances are that you got an A grade in your high school history exam! But the first American to die in the war against the British for American independence was a black man named Crispus Attucks, and the traffic lights system now used all over the modern world was invented by a black American named Garret A. Morgan.'

Tony Brown goes on to inform his listeners that the first ever successful open heart surgery was carried out by a black doctor named Daniel Hale Williams in Chicago in 1893 and that millions have had their lives saved by blood plasma because of a black doctor named Charles Drew. So if the achievements of black people are not recorded by *us*, we must not be surprised if no one else bothers to record them, and it continues to be taken for granted that the only things black people are good at are running, jumping, boxing and singing!

Every person in this country should read the book *Black Pioneers of Science and Invention* by Louis Haber, published in 1970 by Harcourt Brace and World Inc. The story of black people in Britain has been recorded by Peter Fryer in *Staying Power*, published by Pluto Press, while the autobiography of Robert Wellesley Cole, the first African to be elected a Fellow by examination of the Royal College of Surgeons of England, is absolutely riveting reading. This last-named is entitled *An Innocent in England* and is published by Campbell Matthews & Co.

A friend of mine who notices these things sent me copies of correspondence he had with *The Times* newspaper and the Press Council when he made a complaint. As he saw it, on 25 July 1985 over 2,500 people, many of them black, crowded into St Paul's Cathedral, London, for the consecration of the first ever black bishop in the Church of England, the established Church of the land. He was mortified that not a single national newspaper reported this event, which he considered to be an important milestone in the history of the Commonwealth, and he felt that *The Times*, as the reputable chronicle of historical events, should have made some mention of this happening. For obvious reasons I mention this incident with some diffidence! I trust our budding historians will take note.

There is still another reason why we must recount again and again the epic struggle of the civil rights campaign and Martin Luther King's role in it.

Last year I read David Garrow's book on Martin Luther King and the civil rights movement for which he was awarded the Pulitzer Prize. It is entitled *Bearing the Cross* and is meticulously researched and written in a scholarly and dispassionate manner. A colleague drew to my attention that just before Christmas one of our English quality newspapers carried what was meant to be a review of this book. It was a strange review, in that the reviewer managed to write more than half of it before he actually mentioned the book. Yet by then he had found space to mention that Martin Luther King's achievement was 'imposing but ambiguous', and also that 'he lived in the daily expectation of being exposed by the FBI for his compulsive sexual adventures'; that 'he was not the sort of man to whom courage was instinctive'; and that 'so far as *de facto* segregation in the South was concerned King and his movement were pushing on an open door!'

Well, if sitting at lunch counters and having chairs broken over your head, as I saw on television, or being attacked by police dogs and beaten with sticks by policemen, and freedom riders being murdered—if all that is pushing on an open door, God only knows what would have happened if that door had been closed. The reviewer goes on to say that 'if King had been confronted, not by racist and demagogic Democrats such as George Wallace, who played into his hands, but by today's two-party system in the South with conservative Republicans in the White House, King might have found it much harder to achieve the results he did.'

Given time, I do not doubt that there will be 'reviewers' and 'historians' to tell us that if the civil rights movement did take place at all it was all the result of a few misguided black people who were really quite happy singing and dancing on Southern plantations, but were bribed into putting on a show for the cameras; that what we saw gushing was not blood at all but red paint; and that the man Martin Luther King had never really existed but was a projection of the messianic hopes of black people.

A biographical note

So, for the record, let me repeat a few facts.

Martin Luther King was born on 15 January 1929 in Atlanta, Georgia, the second of three children of The Revd Martin Luther King Senior and his wife Alberta. This was less than 70 years after the abolition of slavery in the South and slavery had been replaced by segregation. Segregation was enforced by the white people who held all the power, made all the rules and disobeyed any laws which did not suit them.

Black life was cheap and any black person who wanted to stay alive and continue to live in the South had to accept the situation as he or she found it. This meant that black people toiled long hours in menial jobs for poor wages and could not use the facilities of hotels, restaurants, schools and churches which white people used. So within the constraints of this second-class existence black people struggled for human dignity in their human activities of loving and caring for their children, looking after their aging parents and their neighbours, worshipping God and valuing human life. They recognized the forces of oppression in their lives as evil and they lived in hopes of a better day. But they had also seen the brutal killing of black people who tried to change things.

An outstanding scholar

As a minister, King's father was a respected figure in the black community and young Martin had a comparatively comfortable childhood. He was an outstanding scholar who combined all the normal enjoyments of a young man exploring and discovering adulthood, with the excitement of new ideas, wider visions, thought and argument, as in his reading and study he engaged with the minds of the great philosophers, both ancient and modern.

At college he loved discussions, music and dancing, was considered a sharp dresser who knew how to 'lay on the threads, man!', and he hung out with the other young bloods of his set. He knew how to enjoy life, and he knew that life was for living. After graduating from Morehouse College with a BA degree in Sociology in 1948, he entered Crozier Theological Seminary and studied for the ministry. He married Coretta Scott in 1954 and that same year became a full-time pastor of Dexter Avenue Baptist Church in Montgomery, Alabama. He continued his studies and in the following year, 1955, was made a Doctor of Philosophy in Systematic Theology by Boston University.

Montgomery bus boycott—a watershed

The Kings' first child was born in November 1955 and in December that year Rosa Perks, a black woman on her way home from work after a hard day, refused to give up her seat on a bus in order to let a white man sit down because she was just too tired. For this she was arrested. The black community in Alabama decided that as a people they were just too tired of being pushed around, and that until they were allowed to sit on the buses on a basis of 'first come, first served' they would not use the buses. Thus began one of the watershed events in American history—the Montgomery bus boycott.

Martin Luther King was then a young minister in his first pastorate; he was newly married with a young child; he was comparatively new to the city and he did not see himself as a leader among ministers (so many of whom were older and more experienced than he) and certainly not as a leader of black people and organizations. But when the ministers and other community leaders met and decided that the time had come to make a stand, it was the young Martin Luther King—who in the short time among them had already impressed them by his learning, his preaching and his leadership of the church—that they chose to be their spokesman.

This is an important point which we should not forget. *Martin Luther King did not make the civil rights movement and he never claimed that he did. The movement made him.*

The Montgomery bus boycott went on for over a year. King was arrested and thrown into jail for driving at 30 miles per hour in a 25 miles-per-hour zone. A bomb was thrown onto the porch of his house while he was at a meeting and his wife and baby and a friend were in the house.

In November 1956 the US Supreme Court declared that the bus segregation laws of Alabama State were illegal and in December the Montgomery city buses were integrated for the first time. It was a noble and notable victory, a costly victory. It was a victory for the entire black community, who had at great inconvenience refused to use the buses for a year, and it vindicted their choice of King as the man to articulate and personify their determination and their courage.

King's courage and dignity

The heroes, men and women, of the civil rights movement are many, and not all their names are recorded. The sheer brutality of those in power in the Southern states, their disregard for human life, decency and law in their efforts to deny black people their rights, caused many Americans, black and white, as well as other decent people from around the world, to rally to the civil rights struggle. King's courage and dignity, his total dedication to the Christian precepts of forgiveness and reconciliation, of confronting evil with good, and his adherence to the practice of non-violence, won the movement many friends and supporters.

People taking part in sit-ins in restaurants that refused to serve black people were beaten by police, attacked and bitten by police dogs, and had clothes torn from their backs by high-pressure water hoses. Freedom-riders and black people trying to register as voters were murdered. King himself was thrown into jail many times; he and his family received threatening telephone calls and letters almost daily. He was spat at, stoned, and once he was stabbed. As more and more people were murdered, angry black people, not part of the movement, began to react violently and rioted; others left the official Southern Christian Leadership Conference to form splinter groups.

Yet Martin Luther King remained constant and faithful to Christian vision and the practice of non-violence. He was tireless in his speaking, preaching and writing. He was realistic and yet he always had the same message to friend and foe alike: 'We shall overcome.' So it was typical of the man that when he was awarded the Nobel Peace Prize in 1964, he pointed out that the award had not been won by him, but by the movement, and that too many injustices still remained.

Inclusive love

King's love for humankind was inclusive, not exclusive. That is why the Poor People's Campaign and his stand against the war in Vietnam followed naturally on his concern for justice for black people. A candle of light was extinguished by the man who murdered Martin Luther King in Memphis, Tennessee on 4 April 1968.

Even a random selection of King's utterances at various times can give us a flavour of his message.

To develop a sense of black consciousness and peoplehood does not require that we scorn the white race as a whole. It is not the race per se *that we fight, but the policies and ideology that leaders of that race have formulated to perpetuate oppression.*

A doctrine of black supremacy is as evil as a doctrine of white supremacy.

The negro cannot win ... if he is willing to sell the future of his children for his personal and immediate comfort and safety.

Freedom is never given by the oppressor, it must be demanded by the oppressed.

The belief that God will do everything for man is as untenable as the belief that man can do everything for himself. It too is based on lack of faith. We must learn that to expect God to do everything while we do nothing is not faith but superstition.

Powerful words indeed.

Impact on those who heard him

The following extract from Maya Angelou's autobiographical book *The Heart of a Woman* will convey to you the impression and impact Martin Luther King made on those who heard him.

The host minister rose again, and all rustling stopped. The room held its breath.

The preacher told us what we already knew about Martin Luther King, the dangers he had experienced and the triumphs he had won. The listeners didn't move. There was a yawping expectancy under the stillness. He was here, our own man, black, intelligent and fearless. He was going to be born to us in a moment. He would stand up behind the pulpit, full grown, and justify the years of sacrifice and the days of humiliation. He was the best we had, the brightest and the most beautiful. Maybe today would be the day we would find ourselves free.

The introduction was over and Martin Luther King, Jr., rose. The audience, collectively, lost its composure, pews scraped against the floor as people stood, rearing back, pushing, leaning forward, shouting.

'Yes, Lord. Come on, Dr. King. Just come on.'

A stout short woman in red, standing next to me, grabbed me around the waist and squeezed. She looked at me as if we were old friends, and whispered, 'If I never draw another breath, I could die happy.'

She released me and caught the arm of a man on her right, pulling the arm to her breast, cradling it and whispering, 'It's all right, now. He's right here and it's all right.'

Martin Luther King, Jr., stood on the dais, away from the podium, allowing the audience full view of his body. He looked at the audience, smiling, accepting the adulation but strangely apart from it. After a minute, he walked to a position behind the podium and raised both hands. It was at once a surrendering and a quelling gesture. The church became quiet, but the people remained standing. They were trying to fill their eyes with the sight of the man.

He smiled warmly and lowered his arms. The audience sat immediately, as if they had been attached by invisible strings to the ends of his fingers.

He began to speak in a rich sonorous voice. He brought greetings from our brothers and sisters in Atlanta and in Montgomery, in Charlotte and Raleigh, Jackson and Jacksonville. A lot of you, he reminded us, are from the South and still have ties to the land. Somewhere there was an old grandmother holding on, a few uncles, some cousins and friends. He said the South we might *remember is gone. There was a new South. A more violent and ugly South, a country where our white brothers and sisters were terrified of change, inevitable change. They would rather scratch up the land with bloody fingers and take their most precious document, the Declaration of Independence, and throw it in the deepest ocean, bury it under the highest mountain, or burn it in the most flagrant blaze, than admit justice into a seat at the welcome table, and fair-play room in a vacant inn.*

Geoffrey and I slid close, until our shoulders and thighs were touching. I glanced at him and saw tears glistening on his dark face.

Rev. King continued, chanting, singing his prophetic litany. We were one people, indivisible in the sight of God, responsible to each other and for each other.

We, the black people, the most displaced, the poorest, the most maligned and scourged, we had the glorious task of reclaiming the soul and saving the honour of the country. We, the most hated, must take hate into our hands and by the miracle of love, turn loathing into love. We, the most feared and apprehensive, must take fear and by love, change it into hope. We, who die daily in large and small ways, must take the demon death and turn it into Life.

His head was thrown back and his words rolled out with the rumbling of thunder. We had to pray without ceasing and work without tiring. We had to know evil will not forever stay on the throne. That right, dashed to the ground, will rise, rise again and again.

When he finished washing us with his words, caressing our scarred bodies with his optimism, he led us in singing 'Oh, Freedom.'

Strangers embraced tightly; some men and women wept openly, choking on sobs; others laughed at the waves of spirit and the delicious tide of emotion.

Maya Angelou, *The Heart of a Woman*, Virago Press, 1986, pages 54–57

Incidentally, Maya Angelou's five books of autobiography, starting with *I Know Why the Caged Bird Sings* (Virago Press) are necessary reading for all conscious black folk. And perhaps for all conscious Christians as well.

That, my sisters and brothers, is the man whose memory and contribution we are honouring tonight. It was God who gave him to us, and those whom God has joined together let no man put asunder.

One of a long line of black heroes

And now, what of ourselves? Giant as he was, Martin Luther King Jr was but one of a long line of black heroes whose contribution lives on in the lives of today's people. They have been inspired by what he and others like him said and did, and it is right that they should be mentioned in any address which touches on the struggle for the freedom and dignity of black people: Albert Luthuli, Malcolm X, Marcus Garvey, W.E.B. Du Bois, Booker T. Washington, George Washington Carver, Harriet Tubman, Sojourner Truth, Toussaint L'Ouverture, Paul Robeson, Nelson Mandela, Steve Biko, Desmond Tutu and many others.

They played their part in the struggle, now we must play ours. The aim is the same, namely, for us as people to take our place equally alongside others in decision making in every sphere—social, political and economic—in the life of the society of which we are a worthy part.

Last year I stressed that we must 'value our hyphen'. Just as there are Welsh-British, Scottish-British, Irish-British and many others, so we can be Black-British or Afro-British with both loyalty and pride.

- *The purpose of this is self-help—caring for elderly people, supporting needy families and so on.*
- *One area of concern should be the unacceptably high number of black people at present in prison.*
- *I also suggested that we should aim for the establishment of one or more Black Cultural Archives centres where young people might go to peruse the records of achievement by black people down through the ages.*

I would repeat what we said then because the need becomes more urgent every day.

A challenge for us today

Each one of us must now take up the challenge on a *personal basis*. Malcolm X used to say that sitting at table did not make him a diner. You could sit at table with the best knife and fork and a napkin the size of a table-cloth on your lap, but if you are not eating you are not a diner!

It is not enough for any black person to know that there is a struggle going on—that does not make him or her part of the struggle. In fact, he or she may be part of the dead weight which is making the struggle so difficult.

We are only people, and like any other group of people we will have among us a small number of geniuses and a certain number of incompetents, but the vast majority of us are of average intelligence, average ability and with a good deal of average common sense.

If every average black person in Britain today was determined to participate consciously in the struggle, the image of black people in this country would change for the better almost overnight. Let me suggest a way forward.

Contributing together to help one another

Years ago in the Caribbean, poor people who worked for low wages devised a way of saving money all together and helping one another at the same time. A group of twelve people or so would each week contribute say five dollars to a common pool making a total of sixty dollars. Then, in strict rotation, this lump sum went to members in turn, which meant that the receiving member was able to make a purchase that week without having to borrow money and pay interest on it.

In Jamaica this was called a 'pardner', in Barbados it was called a 'meeting-turn' and in Trinidad and some other islands it was called a 'Sou-sou'. Out of this grew the more sophisticated credit union movement, which I am pleased to say has taken root in this country and has been a great help to many of us. I remember that some years ago, when the old car I was driving fell apart and left me sitting on the engine, I was able to go to my credit union—the Shepherd's Bush Credit Union—and borrow a thousand pounds for a replacement. As you will know, the principle on which a credit union works is that members must already have something in common—for example the same work-place, or the same church or the same club.

Forming 'King's Groups'

I would suggest that we now invoke the same idea, not for sharing *money* but for self-help activity in the community. Groups of people who know each other or have something in common—a common profession, or neighbourhood, work-place or church should form in order to undertake a piece of work helpful to the community either in the short-term or in the long run.

Membership of these 'King's Groups' should never exceed twelve in number, and I am sure that our own group (which sponsored this evening's activities) would be only too pleased to keep a register of such groups if that was thought desirable.

The specific task which any one group would undertake might grow out of the experience or interest of a member of the group, but once adopted by the group would become the responsibility of the whole group.

Let me remind you that this is for ordinary, average people, and I would plead with you all not to wait for someone else to invite you to join a group. As soon as you reach home tonight, get a piece of paper and write down the names of eleven other people you would want to be in a group with. Then tomorrow begin telephoning them.

You can begin by telling them how enjoyable this evening has been and that next year we are planning something even better. Tell them about the idea of the 'King's Groups' and give them a week to think about it. Then, next Sunday, you call them again to see how many have agreed and arrange to get your first get together. If we are *all* to overcome, each one of us has to undertake.

I would end with the story of the donkey who was standing exactly half-way between two equally desirable pails of water. He could either choose one and go for it, or he could fail to make up his mind, remain where he was and die of thirst. Which is it to be for us?

Section Two

The Faith

8

THE MESSAGE OF CHRISTMAS

Given at some of the carol concerts in the Fairfield Hall, Croydon

Each year, at the packed-out carol concert given by the Croydon Philharmonic Society in the Fairfield Hall, Bishop Wilfred Wood is invited to give a five-minute Christmas message. Here are just four of them.

Emmanuel, God with us

Perhaps you have heard of the small boy who was writing a letter to Jesus about his Christmas present. 'Dear Jesus,' he wrote, 'If you get me a bike for Christmas, I promise not to be naughty or get into trouble for a whole year.' Then he thought for a while and changed 'a whole year' to 'six months'. He thought again, and changed 'six months' to 'six weeks'. Finally, he looked around and saw a statue of the Virgin Mary. He put the statue in a drawer, locked the drawer and put the key in his pocket. Then he began his letter a second time: 'Dear Jesus, if you want to see your mother again . . .'

Like that little boy we would all like to receive gifts that would make us happy, but we would like to receive them without any obligation on our part. And sometimes, when we pursue our own happiness at all costs, we end up threatening others or even hurting them. That is why, in addition to all the suffering in the world caused by such tragedies as the earthquake in Armenia, the floods in Bangladesh and the hurricane in Jamaica, we have the unnecessary suffering resulting from conflict between human beings—between Israeli and Palestinian in the Middle East, white and black in South Africa, between Protestant and Catholic in Northern Ireland. This all happens because each of us thinks too highly of himself or herself and too little of other people.

Christmas shows us how wrong this is. Christmas shows the dignity and worth of human personality. For what we are celebrating at Christmas is nothing less than the action of God in coming to live among men and women in a world which he himself had created. He chose to give himself to the world with no strings attached. So he was born to a woman who was homeless at the time, and in a stable filled with the stench of animals, because that was the only shelter she could find.

You cannot get lower than that, and this tells us that God's presence is not dependent upon pomp and circumstance, but is seen in human beings at their most vulnerable—human beings who are without homes, families or friends such as refugees or tramps who are mentally or physically handicapped; sick or dying; in prison or in bereavement.

Because God loves humankind, he came to us in a form that did not threaten us, but rather in a form that speaks to the best that is within us. We best show our love for him by respecting other human beings, no matter how weak and vulnerable they are, and seeing them as equally precious, with us, in his sight. This is the lesson of Christmas.

God bless us all this Christmas, and forgive and restore us when we fail in love.

> Dear friends, let us love one another, for love comes from God. Everyone who loves has been born of God and knows God. Whoever does not love does not know God, because God is love. This is how God showed his love among us: He sent his one and only Son into the world that we might live through him. This is love: not that we loved God, but that he loved us and sent his Son as an atoning sacrifice for our sins. Dear friends, since God so loved us, we also ought to love one another. No-one has ever seen God; but if we love one another, God lives in us and his love is made complete in us...
>
> We love because he first loved us. If anyone says, 'I love God,' yet hates his brother, he is a liar. For anyone who does not love his brother, whom he has seen, cannot love God, whom he has not seen. And he has given us this command: Whoever loves God must also love his brother.
>
> 1 John 4:7–12, 19–21 (NIV)

The Prince of Peace

At Christmas time, when we celebrate the birth of Jesus, we hear him described as the Prince of Peace. This is because, long before he came, the prophets had said that God wanted a world in which there would be no war.

The prophet Micah said that in the days to come nations would hammer their swords into ploughshares, would never again train for war, and every man would sit at peace under his own vine and fig tree. The belief was that the coming of Christ would introduce this era of peace.

Christ has come, and yet we do not have peace. One reason for this is described in the words of the late Martin Luther King. He said:

The belief that God will do everything for man is as untenable as the belief that man can do everything for himself. That, too, is based on lack of faith. We must learn that to expect God to do everything while we do nothing is not faith but superstition.

We human beings have not played our part in this joint venture of establishing peace. We *say* we have faith in God, but in *practice* our faith is in nuclear weapons and a huge and expensive military machine to keep the peace.

We are like the woman in church who always bowed low whenever the name of Jesus was mentioned. But it was noticed that she bowed equally low whenever the name of Satan was mentioned. When asked about this strange behaviour she explained: 'Well, I don't know whose hands I shall fall into when I die. So I am making friends on both sides.'

Jesus knew that true peace can never be established by armed strength. He knew that peace is the fruit of justice. That is why, when the messengers from John the Baptist came to ask him if he was indeed the person to introduce God's kingdom of peace, he told the messengers to look for signs of such a kingdom. Were the sick being healed? Were the poor being treated with dignity and respect? Was the gospel being proclaimed?

Every Christmas is a reminder that God is again inviting us to join in bringing about peace on earth. We might respond to his invitation in three ways.

First, we must pray for peace.

Secondly, we know that if poor Third World countries were to reduce their arms expenditure by only half, all the children in the Third World could have access to clean water and primary education. Since these arms are manufactured here and sold to these poor countries, we must press our politicians to end this trade, and so force these countries to find other means of resolving their differences.

Thirdly, there are many people in our society who are ill-equipped to win for themselves the just treatment to which their God-given human dignity entitles them. For example people dying of Aids, and people in our prisons who know that other people know them to be innocent but choose to do nothing about it; and people such as asylum-seekers who flee for their lives from murderous tyrants overseas only to find that they are refused refuge here.

If we are to help the prince of peace establish peace on earth we must, each of us, work for justice—for peace is the fruit of justice.

May God bless us all this Christmas and always.

In the last days the mountain of the Lord's temple will be established as chief among the mountains; it will be raised above the hills, and peoples will stream to it.

Many nations will come and say,

'Come, let us go up to the mountain of the Lord, to the house of the God of Jacob. He will teach us his ways, so that we may walk in his paths.' The law will go out from Zion, the word of the Lord from Jerusalem. He will judge between many peoples and will settle disputes for strong nations far and wide. They will beat their swords into ploughshares and their spears into pruning hooks. Nation will not take up sword against nation, nor will they train for war any more. Every man will sit under his own vine and under his own fig-tree, and no-one will make them afraid, for the Lord Almighty has spoken. All the nations may walk in the name of their gods; we will walk in the name of the Lord our God for ever and ever...

'But you, Bethlehem Ephrathah, though you are small among the clans of Judah, out of you will come for me one who will be ruler over Israel, whose origins are from of old, from ancient times...'

He will stand and shepherd his flock in the strength of the Lord, in the majesty of the name of the Lord his God. And they will live securely, for then his greatness will reach to the ends of the earth. And he will be their peace.

Micah 4:1–5; 5:2, 4–5 (NIV)

Peace on earth

Sometimes the words we sing in our songs or hymns or carols are denied by our actions. Years ago one of my fellow curates used to amuse us with his take-off of an incident he had witnessed. The head teacher of our local primary school was a lovely Christian lady, but she was also a very strict disciplinarian, and one day as she was leading the children in a song about Jesus, she caught sight of a child near her being naughty. So she went—'Jesus' hands are kind hands, doing good to all'—*SMACK!*

One of our popular Christmas carols includes these beautiful but sad words:

And man at war with man hears not
The love song which they bring.
Oh hush the noise ye men of strife
And hear the angels sing...

I believe that if each of us was suddenly given just half a minute to answer the question, 'What is the message of Christmas?' most of us would immediately reply, 'Peace on earth and good will towards men'—unless of course we are feminists, in which case we would say 'men and women'.

This year, Christmas comes in the middle of the Gulf crisis, a crisis precipitated by Saddam Hussain's invasion of Kuwait. It was an illegal act and Iraq now illegally occupies other people's territories. Other countries in that region have done the same and the United Nations have equally and unanimously condemned all such invasions and called for a complete withdrawal from such illegal occupation.

But it has been depressing during the past few months to see how we are being conditioned to accept the possibility of war as a means of securing Iraq's withdrawal. There is nothing good about war. Even professional soldiers, who earn their livelihood by being trained to defend their country, have wives and children and should not lightly be asked to give their lives. For a war of this kind will not be fought with bows and arrows, and it could result in hundreds and perhaps thousands of children growing up in this country without fathers. When the millionaire owners of the tabloid newspapers which are presently inciting us all to war have cried all the way to the bank, the legal wrangles to secure reasonable provision for widows and orphans will then have to begin.

We must heed the message of Christmas. No one nation—not even America—has all the truth, justice and goodwill that there is in the world, and some of these may even be in Iraq. Our Christ is the prince of peace and we should be peace-loving—not sometimes, but at all times. So let us pray for both Presidents Bush and Hussein, that as they look on the Christ-child in the manger this Christmas they will see in the face of the Christ-child the faces of the thousands of babies who may not live to see another Christmas, if war, and not peace, comes to the Gulf at this time. God bless you this Christmas, and always.

The gift of God

In the school's nativity play the first of the three kings approached the manger, bowed and presented his gift.

'Gold', he said, and withdrew.

The second king approached, bowed and presented his gift.

'Myrrh', he said.

The third king approached, bowed, presented his gift and announced: 'Frank sent this!'

We do not know who Frank was, but we do know that he was generous because he sent a gift.

Each Christmas we celebrate the arrival of a gift to humankind from God our Father. It is the gift of life, of love and of salvation in the life, death and resurrection of Jesus Christ. But it begins with a gift—as a reminder that everything begins with God, he always takes the first step. When God comes to us, he chooses to come in weakness and vulnerability, in a non-threatening form in order that we may be our true selves in responding to him, free of fear and anxiety. He knows that whenever we respond to him in a way that reflects his own nature we are our better selves. So generosity will triumph over greed, sacrifice over selfishness, goodwill over indifference.

That first Christmas he came in the form of a vulnerable baby, whose unmarried mother could not make proper provision for his arrival because she was away from home.

Ever since that first Christmas he has been coming to us in the weakness and vulnerability of the human beings he loves so much.

In Ethiopia and the rest of the Two-Thirds World where, every minute of every day, eighteen children die of starvation, he comes to us.

In frail, elderly people shut away from the eyes of a busy world, he comes to us.

In the frightened, exploited Pakistani and other immigrants, he comes to us.

He does not want us to fear him—any more than we fear the tiny Christ-child in the manger. But he does want us to love him, because he first loved us.

9

CHRISTMAS SERMON

Given at Midnight Mass, St Laurence, Catford, Christmas 1977

Jesus returned to Galilee in the power of the Spirit, and news about him spread through the whole countryside. He taught in their synagogues, and everyone praised him.

He went to Nazareth, where he had been brought up, and on the Sabbath day he went into the synagogue, as was his custom. And he stood up to read. The scroll of the prophet Isaiah was handed to

> him. Unrolling it, he found the place where it is written:
>
> 'The Spirit of the Lord is on me, because he has anointed me to preach good news to the poor. He has sent me to proclaim freedom for the prisoners and recovery of sight for the blind, to release the oppressed, to proclaim the year of the Lord's favour.'
>
> Then he rolled up the scroll, gave it back to the attendant and sat down. The eyes of everyone in the synagogue were fastened on him, and he began by saying to them, 'Today this scripture is fulfilled in your hearing.'
>
> Luke 4:14–21 (NIV)

What we are celebrating is the biggest thing that has ever happened in the world, known in religious language as the incarnation. That is to say, the one God who created the moon and the budgerigar, the sun and the goldfish, the planets of the universe and the common house-fly, also devised a means whereby we human beings might know what he is like, and ourselves be empowered to share in his nature.

The means he devised was to become human like ourselves. Now every man and woman born as a child into this world—whether the birth is attended by the best medical brains on earth, or whether the mother is on her own in a mud hut with no water, either hot or cold—has a share in God himself.

We must know, from the life of Our Lord Christ, from his birth, through death to resurrection, that God is self-giving love, so that when we speak of the crucifixion of Jesus, or the resurrection of Jesus, or the birth of Jesus, we are speaking of the flashpoints of this one and same revelation. They are all windows opening on the spectacle of the eternal love of God.

It was the Church who chose 25 December as an occasion for calling to mind the birth of Our Lord, but I wonder if the Fathers of the early Church could have foreseen that this one day would be so wrenched out of its proper context that in our day people now look forward to Christmas, but refuse to be followers of Christ. People insist on holidays but do not observe holy days; people celebrate with food and drink but do not celebrate the Eucharist with the bread and wine which are the body and blood of Christ.

I doubt if those early Fathers could have foreseen that a television executive would apologize for having to have religious programmes on Christmas Day because it fell on a Sunday, or that parents of school-children would object because a headmaster allowed his religious principles to affect Christmas observance.

So the Fathers of the Church were wise indeed that in choosing 25 December they were careful to make it only one of a cluster of holy days: 25 December, the birth of Christ; 26 December, the murder of St Stephen, the first man to be killed because he was a Christian; 27 December, St John the Apostle, the only one of Our Lord's Apostles to live to a ripe old age, and 28 December, the Holy Innocents' Day—those babies who were slaughtered by King Herod in his effort to do away with Jesus.

So for some people, Christmas may be nothing more than a family festival or a national cultural occasion, but for us Christians it has to be more than that and we are grateful for this cluster of saints' days. These three days show us examples of what Christ coming among us could do to make men like himself. They show that his blessing is not limited to any one way of serving him, or to any one kind of person, but is meant for all sorts and conditions and ages, and that he, in his love and mercy, has a place in his kingdom for young and old, great and small. His Church is not a human company or college or army where only a particular sort of person is wanted and picked out. He takes all sorts who stand in need of his grace. The fruits of his incarnation will be seen, not in one class or race of humankind, but in every variety of humankind.

Here we are reminded that there are many different ways of serving Christ, and different ways of glorifying him, provided we are faithful to him. Some of God's saints today will be, like Stephen, young men who are cut off in their prime but who have established, for Christ and his Church, service that could have taken a lifetime. Others may be like St John, living patiently through a long and perhaps weary life, year by year seeing old friends die or disappear, having to get used to new ways and new faces, serving Christ in a quiet and almost monotonous way.

And what about today's children, born to die before they are two years old? Struck down not by the sword of a cruel king but by the disease and poverty and starvation forced upon their parents by cruel and oppressive tyrants and governments? And children also murdered even before they are born, to suit the convenience of selfish and greedy individuals. The Innocents' Day with its proximity to Christmas Day is a reminder of the depths to which a world without Christ's love can sink.

St John was above all the apostle of love. It was he who has recorded for us some of Our Lord's best-loved sayings, such as, 'This is my commandment, that you love one another as I have loved you.' And again, 'A new commandment I give you: that you love one another.'

It is St John also who has told us that Christ said, 'As the Father has loved me, so I have loved you,' and 'God so loved the world that he gave his only begotten Son, that whosoever believeth on him should not perish but have everlasting life.'

In later years St John himself reflected the sentiments of his master: 'My little children, let us not love in word, neither in tongue, but in deed and in truth.' And again, 'God is love, and he that dwells in love, dwells in God, and God in him.' And finally, 'We know that we have passed from death to life, because we love the brethren.'

These three pointers indicate what the Christian life is about and what Christianity should mean to Christians:

- ***The centrality of love depicted by St John.***
- ***Faithfulness even unto death, illustrated by St Stephen.***
- ***Suffering which we did not choose and do not understand as seen in the slaughter of the Innocents.***

We Christians should never consciously or even unconsciously adopt a holier-than-thou attitude to other people. Nor should we begrudge them the warmth, heartiness and backslapping of Christmas time. But we do believe that Christianity is the religion of the incarnate Son of God, and that this has implications for those of us who are his followers. Because we are called upon to live out our faith in a world that has gone wrong we cannot order our priorities or select our morals on the basis of a majority vote. Nor are we so presumptuous as to assume that non-Christians must adopt a Christian stance in private or public morals or politics. But we Christians ought to know what course we ought to take because of the life we are living.

Our purpose in life is now Christ's purpose, and to make clear this purpose to us, by word and by example, Christ came to us at Christmas. He spelt it out in the first sermon that he preached on his return to Nazareth where he had been brought up.

'The Spirit of the Lord is upon me because he has anointed me; he has sent me to announce good news to the poor, to proclaim release for prisoners and recovery of sight for the blind; to let the broken victims go free, and to proclaim the year of the Lord's favour.'

Tonight, as we come forward to share the body and blood of Our Lord, let us pray for our Christian brothers and sisters everywhere, and particularly for those who bear in their own souls and in their persons the marks of innocent suffering (like the Holy Innocents), of faithfulness unto death (like St Stephen) and yet struggle to love (like St John) even in the prison camps and detention centres around the world.

10

MOTHERING SUNDAY

Sermon preached on Mothering Sunday 1979 at St Laurence, Catford

> While Jesus was speaking thus, a woman in the crowd called out, 'Happy the womb that carried you, and the breasts that suckled you!' He rejoined, 'No, happy are those who hear the word of God and keep it.'
>
> Luke 11:27–28 (NEB)

Long before the world of commerce hit upon the idea of Mother's Day, the Church had chosen a day, 25 March, the Feast of the Annunciation, on which to give thanks to God for motherhood, in the person of the Blessed Virgin Mary—the greatest mother in the history of the world. This unique woman stands high in the esteem of Christians, because there can be no doubt of her humanity—she was a woman, and a woman of her times—and it was through her that God chose to take human nature. Holy Scripture records only a few instances of the patience, the trust, the concern and the suffering which were the expression of her continuous and unfailing love for her son, but we may be sure that there were many more. For example, we hear her patiently asking the twelve-year-old Jesus, who had missed the caravan by staying on too long in the temple, 'Son, why have you treated us like this? Your father and I have been searching for you in great anxiety.'

Then at the wedding feast in Cana-in-Galilee, when he seems to be telling her to mind her own business, she still trusts him so much that she tells the servants: 'Do whatever he tells you.' On another occasion she is worried when he spends all day teaching without any pause for refreshment. Finally she keeps vigil at the foot of the cross as his lifeblood pours from the wounds in his hands, feet and side. Mary, the great mother, knew the extreme ecstasies and the extreme pain of motherhood—the gain and the loss of a child.

So every human being—woman and man alike—stands in her debt, for we are not to know what would have been the fate of the world had she said 'no' to the call from God to be the mother of the world's saviour. I remember an elderly priest who gave us in a sermon a picturesque and memorable description of the Annunciation. He used to say that as the full implications of what the angel Gabriel had said dawned upon Mary, all the angels stood on tiptoe to hear what she would say!

So we do not sing the praises of the Blessed Virgin Mary simply because she was a woman, or because she was a mother, or because she was too timid a creature to say 'no' to God. We honour her because she demonstrated in her own person that perfect response to the will of God after which every human being should strive—'Here am I, God: Thy will be done.' It was the same point that Christ made to that woman in the crowd who shouted out: 'Your mother is a lucky woman,' and he replied: 'No luckier than any other woman who hears and obeys God's word to her.'

God calls some women to serve him in motherhood, and some he calls to serve him in ways that do not include motherhood. St Paul was not specially partial to women as such, but writing to the Galatians he had this to say:

> **There is neither Jew nor Greek, there is neither slave nor free, there is neither male nor female; for you are all one in Christ Jesus.**
>
> Galatians 3:28 (RSV)

Here he was stating a basic Christian belief, namely the dignity and worth of human personality. He was not concerned to deny that there are biological differences or differences of temperament between men and women, but he was certainly concerned to deny that these differences made them superior or inferior to one another. All people, whatever their function or their gender, are first and foremost *persons*, and every person is someone for whom Christ has died. We may be sure, from Our Lord's own teaching and example, that this too was his view, so it is all the more astounding that it has taken us so long to follow his example in this respect.

For the truth is, that no matter what lip service we pay to the idea of equality of the sexes, and women's rights, we are reluctant to move away from established patterns which put most women in a position of disadvantage. It is true that there are some things which only women can do! Only women can give birth, for example, but the world would be a poorer place if this is *all* they did. And important as childbearing is, there are many women who have never borne children, but whose contribution towards making the world more loving, more compassionte and altogether more fit for human beings to live in can never be evaluated.

It isn't only that people like Mother Teresa of Calcutta come to mind, but how can we ever tell which has made the greater contribution—the son or daughter who has left home to begin their own families, or the unmarried daughter who has remained at home to nurse first one parent, then the other, to ensure that their last days in this world were as dignified and comfortable as possible, setting, in the process, an example of personal sacrifice which is so much the hallmark of true Christian vocation? Nor is there anything surprising about the fact that even today, in every church congregation it is the women who outnumber the men and bear the brunt of the Church's work and witness. This is no new thing. Luke 8:1–3 actually records the names of the women who followed Jesus and helped to finance his teaching trips.

Now some of us make a point in our prayers for other people not to use the word 'specially' as though we are asking God to give priority to the people we are concerned about. Instead, we use the word 'particularly', because the people we know and name before God are particular examples of many others like themselves whose names we do not know, but for whom we also ask God's healing touch. In the same way today, Mothering Sunday, we give thanks to God for the love of mothers, but not only for the love of mothers. The love a mother has for her child, and the love a child has for her mother, are not *two* loves, different in kind from the love of God! Both are particular expressions of God's everlasting and universal love! Mother and child are carriers of God's love, and they pass this love to one another.

When I was a student in theological college, there was one of our number who, regrettably, was not very good at passing things at table. We used to say that when he was sitting in the middle it was an SOS service—stretch or starve!

Mothers mediate God's love to their children, so that they are neither starved of love, nor in stretching for it damage or destroy other people's lives. That is why the characteristic of such love is *sacrifice*—the voluntary self-giving of the stronger for the good of the weaker. At the start of the relationship it is the mother who is stronger and who must deny herself in order that the weak infant may have the security in which to grow into a mature and responsible human being. Then the roles are reversed, and it is the offspring who must care for the ageing parent to ensure that she prepares for the life hereafter in dignity and peace and with a quiet mind.

Such must be our Christian approach to parenthood. Not at all the same as treating children like display objects whose expensive toys, pastimes and achievements make us the envy of our neighbours and serve as substitutes for the time we should be spending with them, teaching them—by word and example—to love God with all their heart, soul, mind and strength, and their neighbour as themselves.

In the same way we in Church and society must not make exaggerated and extravagant gestures to mothers on one day of the year, Mothering Sunday, if we are going to undervalue them on the 364 other days. If we do we shall be like the children who exclaimed, 'Mother, you shouldn't be washing dishes on Mother's Day! Leave them till tomorrow!'

Mary, the greatest mother of them all, was a humble village girl from a background even more humble than our own. Yet generations of Christians have called her blessed because she said 'yes' to God's call to her. God continues to call men and women to his service, and some of us, like Mary, will be called to suffer. But who knows to what extent God's kingdom will be advanced, if whatever the circumstances we can manage, like her, to say: 'Behold the servant of the Lord. Be it unto me according to your word'?

Let us pray that we may both *hear* the Word of God, and *do* it.

11

MAUNDY THURSDAY

Sermon preached at St Laurence, Catford on Maundy Thursday 1977

The deliberate assembly of Christians for the Eucharist and our taking of bread and wine, giving thanks, breaking and sharing, is rightly called a celebration, because basically it is cause for joy. At every celebration we recount the mighty acts of our Lord's birth, his death, resurrection and ascension through which he expressed his love for us and won for us the benefits we now enjoy.

Even from a purely human, selfish point of view, how can we help being happy at being given so much at so little cost to ourselves? So every Eucharist is a celebration whether it be a grand affair in the open air with thousands of communicants and hundreds of priests, or whether a single priest is joined in a prison cell by a man who is shortly to die. In essence each act has the same timeless character of celebration and a quality not enhanced or diminished by the circumstances. So our Eucharist this evening is the same as our Sunday-by-Sunday and day-by-day celebrations.

But the *occasion* of our celebration this evening—as distinct from the *cause*—is the Last Supper Our Lord shared with his disciples before he died. The words he used then, which have since become so familiar to us, are recorded by St Paul in 1 Corinthians 11:

For I received from the Lord what I also delivered to you, that the Lord Jesus on the night when he was betrayed took bread, and when he had given thanks, he broke it, and said, 'This is my body, which is for you. Do this in remembrance of me.' In the same way also the cup, after supper, saying, 'This cup is the new covenant in my blood. Do this, as often as you drink it, in remembrance of me.'

1 Corinthians 11:23–25 (RSV)

We could meditate on those words for the rest of our lives and still find in them fresh and inspiring insights into Our Lord's relationship with us. We see, for example, that he is alluding to the ancient custom by which a solemn agreement or undertaking was made valid by the sacrifice of an animal. It was this custom which had enabled religious people to recognize the prophetic description of the Servant of the Lord who died for others.

So the idea of sacrifice had passed into *self*-sacrifice as a personal and moral act. So Our Lord is saying that in order that this new covenant should become effective, he was voluntarily taking a course which would lead to his death. Further, for the disciples to share in the cup with him was a demonstration of solidarity with him, both as beneficiaries of his sacrifice and also as being themselves committed to a similar self-offering. This is the true character of the people of God.

It is right that as, fretting at our human limitations, we strain every fibre of our being to express our solidarity with Christ, we call upon every vehicle of human expression—speech, music, art, drama—and the momentous occasion of the Last Supper provides ample scope for these.

So, this service ended, we shall carry out a symbolic action as we in solemn procession make our way to the chapel, and there keep a watch before the Blessed Sacrament throughout the night, calling to mind our Lord's own sleepless night before his crucifixion. Even so, we must remain conscious that it is in the reality of the everyday, workaday world that our solidarity with Christ in self-sacrifice and in service to others must be lived out. We must remain conscious that for many of our fellow Christians, in places like Uganda, Rhodesia, Lebanon and Northern Ireland, such ritual and symbolic solidarity is a mere nothing alongside the real self-sacrifice that their solidarity demands.

What is more, their solidarity and ours, far apart as they may be, will both have their limitations. Just as a person about to board a plane for a long journey can be accompanied to a certain point by his friends and after that must make his way alone, so the very togetherness of Christ and his disciples at the Last Supper was a reminder that the task ahead of him was one that he had to undertake alone.

Yet his thoughts were not of himself and the terrible ordeal that lay ahead of him, but of them and of their comparatively minor worries. He knew that they would be bewildered by the events that were to take place, that they would feel lost without him. So he sets out to comfort them. 'Let not your hearts be troubled; you believe in God, believe also in me.'

And again, 'There is much that I could say to you, but the burden would be too great for you.' And yet again, 'I have told you all this, so that in me you may find peace. In the world you will have trouble. But be of good cheer—I have overcome the world.'

He was right. And because he was proved right, you and I can think of his suffering and his death—and celebrate!

12

GOOD FRIDAY

Sermon preached in Southwark Cathedral on Good Friday 1990

He was despised and rejected by men, a man of sorrows, and familiar with suffering. Like one from whom men hide their faces he was despised, and we esteemed him not.

Surely he took up our infirmities and carried our sorrows, yet we considered him stricken by God, smitten by him, and afflicted. But he was pierced for our transgressions, he was crushed for our iniquities; the punishment that brought us peace was upon him, and by his wounds we are healed. We all, like sheep, have gone astray, each of us has turned to his own way; and the Lord has laid on him the iniquity of us all.

Isaiah 53:3–6 (NIV)

They were on their way up to Jerusalem, with Jesus leading the way, and the disciples were astonished, while those who followed were afraid. Again he took the Twelve aside and told them what was going to happen to him. 'We are going up to Jerusalem,' he said, 'and the Son of Man will be betrayed to the chief priests and teachers of the law. They will condemn him to death and will hand him over to the Gentiles, who will mock him and spit on him, flog him and kill him. Three days later he will rise.'

Then James and John, the sons of Zebedee, came to him. 'Teacher,' they said, 'we want you to do for us whatever we ask.'

'What do you want me to do for you?' he asked.

They replied, 'Let one of us sit at your right and the other at your left in your glory.'

'You don't know what you are asking,' Jesus said. 'Can you drink the cup I drink or be baptised with the baptism I am baptised with?'

'We can,' they answered.

Jesus said to them, 'You will drink the cup I drink and be baptised with the baptism I am baptised with, but to sit at my right or left is not for me to grant. These places belong to those for whom they have been prepared.'

When the ten heard about this, they became indignant with James and John. Jesus called them together and said, 'You know that those who are regarded as rulers of the Gentiles lord it over them, and their high officials exercise authority over them. Not so with you. Instead, whoever wants to become great among you must be your servant, and whoever wants to be first must be slave of all. For even the Son of Man did not come to be served, but to serve, and to give his life as a ransom for many.'

Mark 10:32–45 (NIV)

We are here to be with Jesus. Jesus alive in his body the Church. Jesus present in the sacrament of the altar. This living Jesus, whose life sustains us now every day, every hour, every minute, once experienced a lingering, painful death by crucifixion. Once a year, on this day, the Church in her liturgy recalls the last few hours of Our Lord's ordeal and in it we try, together and as individuals, by prayer and meditation, to enter as fully as we can into Our Lord's suffering and make our own humble and inadequate offering.

Today, neither you the listener nor I the speaker should be the focus of our thoughts. That must be Christ—Christ on the cross. So I invite you now to close your eyes and with your mind's eye picture Jesus on the cross while we recall St Augustine's meditation on the crucifixion.

Look thou upon the wounds of Him who hangeth,
The blood of him who dieth,
the price paid by him who redeemeth thee.
His head is bent to kiss

His arms set wide to embrace
His heart laid open to love
His whole body laid out to redeem.
Think thou what great things are these.
Weigh them in the balance of thy heart
That he may be fixed whole in thy heart
Who for thy sake was fixed whole upon the tree.

Now, however much you and I may desire to appreciate the suffering of Jesus on the cross, you and I are culturally handicapped. In our culture, moderation is held in such high esteem that extremism is thought of as evil. Indeed, it is enough to condemn anyone to label them as extremist. Yet everything about the death of Jesus is extreme. For him it was the extreme price paid for his extreme commitment.

There is injustice when an innocent person is mistakenly convicted. There is extreme injustice when the innocent is convicted not by mistake but deliberately. So it was with Jesus.

Even death can be made more extreme—by combining it with torture. Those of us who have read or heard Dr Sheila Cassidy speak about the experiences of torture victims in Chile, or seen and heard black Africans describe their treatment in detention in South Africa, may just sense a little of this degradation. Crucifixion is torture. So it was with Jesus.

And there is a method of making death by torture more extreme. By making it a public spectacle so that the death-throes of the victim provide entertainment or warning for onlookers. For example, in the war against the Mau Mau in Kenya a mobile gallows was built so that prisoners could be hanged in their home districts as an example to others.

In addition to this extreme physical suffering there was for Jesus the spiritual suffering. If it is true that only the spiritually mature can feel the full weight of moral evil, the burden on Jesus defies description. No wonder he could not choke back the accusatory cry: 'My God, my God, why hast Thou forsaken Me?' What could be more extreme than to accuse the Father, who cannot be other than true to himself, of deserting his beloved Son?

If Thou, O God, the Christ didst leave,
In Him, not Thee, I do believe;
To Jesus dying all alone,
To His dark Cross, not Thy bright Throne,
My hopeless hands will cleave.

But if it was Thy love that died,
Thy voice that in the darkness cried,
The print of nails I long to see,
In Thy hands, God, who fashioned me.
Show me Thy pierced side.

Edward Shillito

> For Christ's love compels us, because we are convinced that one died for all, and therefore all died. And he died for all, that those who live should no longer live for themselves but for him who died for them and was raised again. So from now on we regard no-one from a worldly point of view. Though we once regarded Christ in this way, we do so no longer. Therefore, if anyone is in Christ, he is a new creation; the old has gone, the new has come! All this is from God, who reconciled us to himself through Christ and gave us the ministry of reconciliation: that God was reconciling the world to himself in Christ, not counting men's sins against them. And he has committed to us the message of reconciliation. We are therefore Christ's ambassadors, as though God were making his appeal through us. We implore you on Christ's behalf: Be reconciled to God. God made him who had no sin to be sin for us, so that in him we might become the righteousness of God.
>
> 2 Corinthians 5:14–21 (NIV)

The cross was, for Jesus, the extreme price paid for extreme commitment. He was totally committed to what he described as the 'kingdom of heaven'. For him this kingdom was no utopian dream. It was realizable here on earth, and its realization was somehow dependent upon a convergence of God's will and the will of humankind.

How else can we explain the very first intercession in the prayer he taught his followers, namely, 'Your kingdom come, Your will be done on earth as it is in heaven'?

Jesus ate, slept and breathed this kingdom. His teaching, his healing and his power were all signs of the kingdom, and he missed no opportunity of inviting his hearers to step out of their reality into his. His reality was something his hearers could comprehend but not accept—so far was it from their own experience and expectation.

If Jesus was to be believed, in this kingdom men and women would all be of equal worth. Ties of blood and of kith and kin would be subordinate to the higher good of doing the will of the Father. Riches, as an encumbrance, would be disposed of. The lame would walk, the dumb speak and the poor would receive good news. Worship would be in spirit and in truth.

He was not pleading for favourable consideration of a new experimental lifestyle. He was claiming that this was God's way and therefore the only valid way. He knew that this meant the overturning of the established order, so he could not have been surprised that the civil powers and the religious authorities would be aligned against him and would seek to silence him. Since he knew nothing of compromise and owed no allegiance to the god 'Moderation', the path he was treading could only end at Calvary. It did.

What is there today that you and I would gladly suffer and die for? The idealizing of moderation and compromise means that suffering in a cause can be dismissed as 'self-inflicted', since it could have been avoided. And holding on to our convictions can sometimes transform us into persons with whom it is too dangerous to be identified. When our convictions run contrary to the status quo, or to the majority opinion, or to the wishes of the powerful, people quickly come to see that we spell trouble.

The disciples ran away from Jesus because he was beginning to smell of death. It was better and safer to be in the crowd where no one could identify them or victimize them.

Every Good Friday the spectacle of Christ on the cross, holding fast to his convictions, is a reminder to today's Christians that being true to Christ may mean being in a minority on many of the great social, moral and ethical questions.

How should wealth be acquired and distributed? Should human life be forfeited for the convenience of society, whether the human life be that of an unborn child, a convicted murderer or an ageing invalid? Can the use of nuclear weapons be justified under any circumstances? Should we seek to make profits and amass wealth by manufacturing and selling weapons of war and encouraging other nations to buy them for use against their neighbours, or for their leaders to use to keep their own people in subjection? Should we as a nation strive to become richer even though our efforts further impoverish those who are already poor?

Every Good Friday has a special message for us respectable Church leaders. As 'managers' of the Church we are expected to manage it within the parameters of convention and popular sentiment in this country.

But Good Friday should remind us that, if it was human sin that brought Jesus to the cross, it was the respectable people who crucified him—the people of well-established traditions, because he asked them to go beyond their traditions. To them, what he was asking was simplistic, unsophisticated and with dangerous rabble-rousing potential. Better that one man should die than the whole nation be put at risk.

Still Jesus continues to ask this of us. But we Church leaders know that although from a safe distance we may profess admiration for an Archbishop Romero or a Martin Luther King or a Desmond Tutu, what is expected of us are the management skills which ensure that compromise and moderation triumph over any unseemly extremism—even the extremism of love.

Yet, from first to last, it is love, extreme love that the cross of Jesus is about. Love for the most lovable and love for the loveless. For the mot lovable in the person of the Father, the creator from whom all good things come! Whose every creative act is an expression of himself and therefore of love.

And love for the loveless. Because the saving work of Christ embraces all humankind, and in this weird and wonderful collection are to be found the very dregs of humanity. The sadists, the torturers, the mass murderers, those with brilliant minds whose every working moment is devoted to finding the most efficient means of killing the greatest number of people. What is more, it includes us. What love could be more extreme than that? Love so amazing, so divine, demands.

13

GOD'S SPECIAL MARK

Easter sermon preached at St Andrew's Parish Church, Half Way Tree, Kingston, Jamaica, Easter Day 1988

> With such a hope as this we speak out boldly...
>
> 2 Corinthians 3:12 (NEB)

St Paul, in that beautiful and familiar chapter of 1 Corinthians 13, says that there are three things that will last as long as the world lasts—faith, hope and love. We are called Christians because we believe Jesus to be the Christ, and we believe this through faith. Jesus taught that God is love, so understandably in our worship there is much reference to faith and love. But what about hope? The Church's great festival of Easter, which we are celebrating today, is essentially a festival of hope.

On British television there is a programme called *The Antiques Roadshow* where specialists are asked to identify various objects, so you see them examining these objects very closely looking for the maker's special mark. That mark—the maker's mark—will identify the object as the genuine article. In all the events of history, and in all the goings on in the world around us, God has a special mark. God's mark is *bringing life out of death.*

Sometimes that mark is to be seen in the affairs of a whole nation. For example, the Hebrew people lived as slaves in Egypt, where they were cruelly ruled and badly treated by the Egyptians. They were allowed to live only in the poorest areas; they did the most menial and the dirtiest jobs, and they were paid little or no wages. Their women-folk had no time to be mothers to their own children, because they had to leave them in the poor areas where they lived, while they went to look after the children of the rich Egyptian women. When the Hebrews complained, they were beaten with whips and driven back to work by fully-armed Egyptian soldiers and policemen.

You may think that I am describing the plight of black people in South Africa today. In fact, what I am giving you is a biblical description of God's people in Egypt hundreds of years before the birth of Christ. Then, when things were at their worst, and there was no sign of change, God sent a message to his oppressed people: 'Leave Egypt and head towards the Red Sea. Trust me, and leave the rest to me.' They did so, and God brought them through the Red Sea to freedom and nationhood. *New life out of death—God's mark.*

One of the loveliest stories to come out of the 1939–45 war is of a church in London, which one Saturday had been made ready for the Harvest Thanksgiving Service next day. Among the harvest gifts of fruit and flowers, someone had brought a sheaf of corn. That night, Hitler's bombers came, and the entire church was reduced to a pile of rubble: stones, broken glass, burnt-out timber. Months passed and spring came. And there, out of all that devastation and rubble, appeared tiny green shoots of corn. *Out of death, new life—God's mark.*

As with nations, as with nature, so also with individuals. And the greatest example, of course, Our Lord Jesus Christ. He was killed in the most horrible way—as a criminal, when he was innocent of any crime. He was nailed to a cross and a spear was stuck into his ribs. He died painfully and horribly. But God raised him from the dead, and he could show himself to his friends. Still bearing the marks of the nails in his hands and feet. Still with the wound made by the spear in his side. But now full of new life. *Life out of death—God's mark.*

So even people who do not share our faith can see why, for us Christians, Easter is not only a festival of joy. It is a festival of hope. And the resurrection of Jesus, at the heart of our Christian religion, makes Christianity a religion of hope. There is no situation, however grim, however bleak, that is beyond God's power to redeem. We can all go down to the grave, and even in the grave we'll make our song: Alleluia, Alleluia! For we are an Easter people, and Alleluia is our song.

As Christians we are not ignorant of the grimness of the world we live in, and we do not take this lightly. We know, for example, that there exists a stockpile of nuclear weapons capable of destroying all human life within a matter of minutes. We know that we live under the shadow of possible nuclear accidents, or the malfunctioning of some device which could trigger a world war—as could evil or incompetent men in positions of power.

We know the power of human sin whenever we see children starving to death in fly-infested camps in Ethiopia; or see the victims of civil war in Angola, Lebanon and Northern Ireland or the dehumanization of people by racial oppression in South Africa, Namibia and elsewhere. So we are not naïve.

And it isn't only what goes on outside ourselves or on a national or international scale. In our individual lives, and on a personal scale, we can have moments of near despair when our personal relationships, our health, our hopes for the future, all seem to be in ruins. What we thought had been built with concrete is but a heap of smouldering debris, and we must stand exposed to the gaze and comment of open enemy and false friends alike.

As if that isn't bad enough, we find ourselves *at odds with the society we live in*, especially if we are hurt by the greed, the selfishness and materialism which others have made their way of life, and we see them rewarded with success.

To make matters worse, we are *at odds with those who are nearest and dearest to us*, especially if we are parents, when their need for independence and self-discovery makes them distant at just the time we need them most to support us in our own insecurity.

And worst of all, we are *at odds with ourselves* because of the great, great gap between the kind of lovable and successful persons we would like to be, and the kind of fallible persons we actually are. When these things descend upon us, our depression can be like the darkness of a tomb. And it was out of a tomb that God brought new life on Easter day.

Around three weeks ago I received a letter from a friend in prison. This is part of what he wrote to me: 'It was when I hit the bottom—stripped of clothes, dignity, individuality and status—that God spoke directly to my soul. There is no place that God is not. To paraphrase a piece I came across three days ago: God shattered my plate-glass life, and now he will take the broken pieces and make wind-chimes. Lent is a special time to be in prison. Resurrection is a *promise*, not a maybe.'

As with individuals, so with nature. And here in Jamaica you have the *poui* tree to remind you that, plain and dull as it may be for many months, the time will come when it will burst into the brightest blooms.

As with individuals and with nature, so also with nations. Last week I received a letter from another friend in Britain. She had been reading the autobiography of a well-known churchman, and she found his final theological position unacceptable in that he suggests that it matters little to faith whether anything in the Gospels is history or not. 'But,' she writes, (and I agree with her) 'there ought, for the health of the human mind, to be some point where the mythopoeic and the historical faculties engage simultaneously and with divine sanction. And I can't quite believe, although I am aware that it is at present fashionable to think so, that a human being in the first century was so unconcerned to know if a thing really happened. If anyone had told *me* that a man had risen from the dead, I think I would at least have said: "Are you *sure?*" rather than, "What wonderful spiritual reverberations that statement arouses!"'

That caused me to reflect that whatever means God had chosen to give this well-known churchman his faith, it could not have been the same means by which most of us in the Caribbean and elsewhere, with a background of slavery and colonial oppression, had experienced it. Certainly speaking out of their experiences, my grandparents in Barbados had made it clear to me that whatever injustices the children of God suffered at the hands of human beings were like the sufferings of Christ on the cross, and as surely as he had suffered the worst that wicked men could do to him and had been raised from the dead, as surely would God's children be vindicated and the freedom they enjoyed in the sight of God would one day also be recognized by those who were presently denying it. That was a promise and fact because of the resurrection.

So then we can understand the exchange that took place in the South African Treason Trials in 1956 between the trial judge and that great Zulu leader and Nobel Peace Prize winner, Albert Luthuli (after whom, incidentally, I felt it a privilege to be able to name one of our three sons). Albert Luthuli had described the great lengths that the ANC had gone to in peaceful protests against the unjust apartheid system—the many petitions, delegations, letters, and representations, all to no avail. 'So there was no hope of change, then?' asked the trial judge. 'There was no *sign* of change, My Lord,' replied Luthuli, 'but always there is *hope*.'

And it was not bravado that put into the mouth of that other Nobel Peace Prize winner, Bishop Desmond Tutu, his defiant words to the Eloff Commission. 'The South African Government are not God. They are but men. Other tyrants before them have bitten the dust. They may get rid of a Tutu, but the Church of God will be here long after they are no more than a footnote on the pages of history.'

The faith of the Church is the faith in the risen Christ on whom our *hope* is founded.

So those of us who work and pray for a just, participatory and sustainable community of women and men round the world will not be discouraged by the seeming triumph of evil over good. Every Easter reminds us that the life in Christ which we share with Peter, James, John and the first apostles; with Stephen, Paul and other saints down the ages; with the millions who came after them from every nation and people under the sun; with the thousands who, through the years, sat in these same pews, knelt at this same altar rail and now rejoice in a great light and on another shore—this life was brought out of death by God who now offers to do the same in every generation of those whom he has called.

So we renew our baptismal vows to show that we humbly and gratefully accept this offer, and pray that he will keep us firm in the hope that he has set before us, so that we and all his children shall be free, and the whole earth live to praise his name.

Alleluia—Christ is risen!

14

PENTECOST

Sermon preached at an open-air ecumenical service on Peckham Rye, London, Whit Sunday 1983

> Whatever gift each of you may have received, use it in service to one another, like good stewards dispensing the grace of God in its varied forms.
>
> 1 Peter 4:10 (NEB)

Today, Whitsunday, the Church all over the world is celebrating God's greatest gift to humankind. With the coming of God's Holy Spirit into the hearts of men and women, God gave us not only new knowledge of himself, new knowledge of things eternal and new knowledge of ourselves, but also the means to light up and to fan this knowledge into faith and love and hope.

God's Holy Spirit purges us of sin and puts new strength, new thoughts and new desires into our hearts. This Spirit forms a link and a bond between God and humankind which no trials or sorrows or losses in this human life can break. What has been given to us is not merely a revelation and unfolding of God's truth, wonderful as that is, but a power in our hearts to take in that truth. When faced with selfishness, greed, envy, lust for power, cruelty, disease, poverty and all the other manifestations of human sin, whatever else the Christian may say, we cannot say, 'There is no alternative!'

So the Christian is a very wealthy person, in things both spiritual and material. In spiritual things we have the *sacraments of the Church* and especially the Holy Communion in which, by our sharing the body and blood of Christ, God gives us a foretaste of life beyond the grave, lived always in his presence, and also here and now strengthens us for the task of daily Christian witness in the circumstances of our own lives.

He has also given us *the holy Scriptures*, the Bible. By reading the Scriptures prayerfully, and by hearing them read, we grow gradually, helped by the circumstances of our own lives, and the moments we can spend in meditation, to become more and more sensitive to the greatness of the character of Our Lord and Saviour Jesus Christ and be changed more and more into his likeness.

Thirdly, he has given us *the Church*—made up of people like ourselves: sometimes depressed and worried, sometimes anxious and self-centred and self-pitying, sometimes even jealous, envious and a trifle bitter. But always, at all times and in all places, loved by him who knows us better than we know ourselves. Moreover, this Church is more than we can see, for it brings us together with millions, who down through the ages have lived lives of faithful witness to the truth of the Gospel of Christ. Within this fellowship, each of us has a place which no one else can fill. These are all spiritual gifts—freely given.

This great gift of God's Holy Spirit, and these gifts of the Spirit—are they a reward to us because we are better or more deserving than other people? Are they given to us for our own good and for nothing else?

It is important to note that this afternoon's Act of Witness is taking place in the context of three significant events. The first is our celebration of God's gift of the Spirit; the second is the current parliamentary elections campaign; and the third is the culmination of this year's Christian Aid Week.

For any thoughtful Christian a most depressing feature of the election campaign is the naked appeal to human greed and acquisitiveness. Candidates are always suggesting to us that the reason why we should vote for them is that they will be better able to get us more money and put us on ahead of our neighbour. We are encouraged to see ourselves competing with our neighbours for wealth and status, and it is better that we should be the strong one and our neighbour the weak one. Even when mention is made of the national interest, this is seen only as 'corporate selfishness', in which the rest of the world is considered important only so far as they help us to get what we want, and to help us to enjoy higher and higher material standards of living.

Another depressing feature is the slapdash attitude to truth. Political parties are prepared to pay a lot of money to professionals who use every available means to disguise or conceal unpalatable facts and to exaggerate favourable impressions. This produces a distortion of truth, and if we believe that truth is of God we must conclude that such distortion is dangerous and potentially evil.

Contrary to this mentality is the Christian approach to life exemplified by Christian Aid Week. Because we recognize the generosity of God to us, we will want to ensure that as far as possible the means of grace available to us are also available to men and women everywhere. So we will want to help with the provision of Bibles and with the training of ministers, so that by word and sacrament others may also come to know Christ and to grow in his love.

But we know that although in the last resort nothing can withstand the power of God's love, certain material afflictions can be deterrents in the way of people's recognition of that love, and among these are disease, hunger and the kind of poverty which destroys self-respect. No one believes that it is within our capacity to banish all poverty, all disease and all illiteracy from the world, but neither are we free to allow such stumbling blocks to remain if they could be removed by some effort on our part.

So, in addition to (not in place of) what we do as individuals in our own neighbourhood and in this country to help those in need, we must help those in countries overseas whose poverty of body and spirit is greater than we will ever see around us. Charity, while beginning at home, must never be allowed to end there. In today's world, over 500 million people suffer from malnutrition, and many others are victims of disease and homelessness, often not by accident but by the political and economic forces which shape their lives and in which they have no say whatsoever.

Over two hundred Orthodox, Anglican and Protestant denominations of the Christian Church in every continent are linked by Christian Aid in a worldwide service to people in need. This service is rendered irrespective of the religions and creeds of the recipients, in the belief that such service is an essential function of the Christian community.

You will recall the incident recorded in the Gospels when some friends of a sick man could not get him to Jesus because of the crowd. So they removed part of the roof and let the man on his bed down through the hole so that he was close to Jesus. Jesus was so impressed by the men's faith that he healed their friend.

God has given us the Spirit. He has shown us the need. By Christian Aid and all other means we must exercise the faith and take the action which brings his love and healing to the world he loves.

15

A BAPTISM

Preached at the Baptism of Ruth Dando in St Laurence, Catford, 4 June 1978

The baptism of a baby highlights two central truths of the Christian gospel. The first is that faith is the *response* of God's saving act, not the condition of it. You and I were not baptized because we have decided to believe; we believe because we have come to know that we have already been encompassed by Christ's redemption. So our decision to believe *follows* from the saving fact—it is not the saving fact itself. That is to say, we are not saved by any decision *we* have taken. On the contrary, while we were weak and helpless, *God took us* and placed *us* within the sphere of the redemption wrought by Christ.

I did not choose to be born into a Christian family. I did not choose to be taken to the font. I could no more have done these things than the paralysed man in the Gospels, whose friends let him down through the roof to be healed by Jesus, could have pushed his way through the crowd. I did not earn the grace which was freely given to me. I did not choose Christ. Christ chose me. And this choice will always remain a mystery—

something for which I can give no rational explanation, but a fact for which I am profoundly thankful. You and I love God because God first loved us. And he did not love us because we first made ourselves lovely people, lovable, attractive, successful people. I am not justified or made righteous by my faith—I believe, because God has made me acceptable to himself. This doctrine, which is a central truth of our apostolic faith, is perfectly symbolized in the baptism of a baby because the important thing is not what *we* do, but what *God* does.

The second truth which a baptism highlights is that in each individual member of his Church Christ expresses himself in a unique way. Some years ago the wife of my fellow curate gave birth to a second son who was the image of their first. Their doctor said to them: 'This one look so much like the other I don't know why you bothered!' But no matter how much two Christians have in common, the circumstances of their ministry and witness can never be exactly the same. So it is worth reminding ourselves of one bit of the symbolism used in this service—the symbolism of the Easter candle.

Although every Sunday is for the Christian Church a weekly celebration of Christ's resurrection, one day a year—Easter Day—is specifically set aside for the re-presentation of Our Lord's resurrection. So the liturgy begins in a completely darkened church to symbolize the seeming victory of evil as Jesus lay in the grave following his death on the cross. Then into this darkened building comes a single light—the Paschal candle, representing Christ. As it advances, the darkness is pushed away and finally overcome by the light as more and more people take light from the light of Christ. And every time a new Christian is made in baptism, he or she receives a light from this same light of Christ. It is the same light, but the corners of the world and the lives of people who will be touched by the light of Christ in Ruth Julia Mary Dando can never be exactly the same as any other.

If I may be excused a personal reference. It is highly unlikely that any of the people standing around the font forty-one years ago in Holy Innocents Parish Church, Barbados, while an elderly English priest, the Reverend Mr Hutchins, baptized a baby—Wilfred—would have envisaged this baptism today. In the same way, none of us can envisage exactly where and how Christ will use his servant Ruth for the building up of his body, the Church. But we can pray that as from today, not because of anything we do, but because of what God has done in Christ, and what he now does in baptism, there shall shine forth such a light, that by God's grace, will never be put out.

16

CONFIRMATION

A sermon given at a confirmation service at All Saints Church, Sanderstead, on 13 February 1986

> Let your bearing towards one another arise out of your life in Christ Jesus.
>
> Philippians 2:5 (NEB)

The vast majority of people in the world would like other people to think well of them. There are many benefits to be gained from having people think well of you. Not only are you likely to be surrounded by friends and admirers, but also your progress through life can be made easier, including the acquisition of the necessities of life, and sometimes even wealth and luxuries. So, understandably, people go to a lot of trouble to make the right impression on other people, and some even pay a lot of money to learn how to speak, how to sit or stand, and how to be photographed. But all these things have to do with *image* or appearance, and they do not require sincerity or truth or belief.

But St Paul, in his letter to the new Christians in Philippi, teaches that this is not the way for us. We also would like people to think well of us but (and much more important) our behaviour must be a true reflection of what we believe. The behaviour of Christians, and their bearing towards other people, will come out of their life in Christ. So what do we know of Christ Jesus, and what is our life in him?

The whole universe, and everything in it, including human life, was created by God, and continues to be upheld by God. The whole human race, with its various ethnic groups, is only a small part of God's creation. But it is an important part, because God chose the human race as the means by which he would show himself to the world he had created and call it to himself. The method he used was to become human at a particular time and place in human history.

We believe that Jesus, a man born in Bethlehem nearly two thousand years ago to a woman named Mary, is the *Christ*, the Son of God.

The Bible, especially the Gospels of Matthew, Mark, Luke and John, tells us about the life, teaching, death and resurrection of Jesus. We know that he taught that God is first and foremost a God of love. He taught that God's love is active, and brings healing and health to those who are sick, freedom to those whose minds and bodies are imprisoned, and forgiveness for all those offences against God and our neighbours which we call sin.

Jesus Christ taught that God's love is more powerful than anything the world can ever know; stronger than pain, suffering or even death itself. He was proved right when his enemies perverted the course of justice by getting him put on trial with made-up charges, convicted him with false evidence, and hanged him on a cross.

When they had done all that to him, God raised him from the dead, so the cross on which he was hanged became a victory sign. Some people still reject the sign, but for some others it is the sign of everything that Christ was and is, and we wear it proudly to show that we believe. We put our trust in him as God's word to us and to the world.

The life of Christ beyond the grave—the life of the risen Christ—the life of the Holy Spirit of Christ—this life is freely available to us believers, and through baptism Christ takes us to himself and by his Holy Spirit lives in us. We are in him, and he is in us.

The essential mark of life in Christ is *sharing*. We share with others the love of Christ; we share with others in his Holy Spirit. To be in Christ does not make us superior or inferior to our brothers and sisters in Christ, but one with them. This brotherhood and sisterhood of persons baptized into Christ is not restricted to people of our own church, or this country or this culture. The half naked, underfed Ethiopian Christian is as much our brother as are those Christians who travel regularly on Concorde and the *Q.E. II*, or those Christians who attend the same Bible study group as we do. And our bearing towards each of them must come out of our life in Christ Jesus.

This life must be sustained, and God gives to us certain specific means by which he sustains our life in Christ. It is for us to use them to draw upon his grace which is now freely available to us.

To begin with, there is the Bible—the holy Scriptures. Some religions are religions of a book. But ours is not one of them. Ours is the religion of a *person*, Jesus Christ. God is a *living* God and the Bible is more than a book of rules. The Bible is a record of God's revelation of himself to human beings in human situations. It is a means of encounter between God and ourselves, and if you really want to know God better and to grow more and more in his love you must learn to listen to what God says to you in regular and prayerful reading of the Scriptures. So do not read the Bible as you would today's newspaper—flipping through its pages in haphazard fashion—but give it a respected place in your day-to-day life.

Equally necessary for sustaining life in Christ is another gift from God—

the Holy Eucharist or Communion. On the night before he was killed, Christ gathered his friends around him. They assembled as a fellowship with him at the centre. He then gave them two instructions. He said, 'There are two ways in which you are to call to mind my presence with you and among you. First, by loving one another as I have loved you.' He then took bread and wine, gave thanks to God, broke the bread, and shared both bread and wine among them. Then he said: 'Do this in remembrance of me.'

So for those of us who love Christ, and rejoice in what he has done for us, the Eucharist is a guaranteed meeting place with Christ. His presence in the Eucharist does not depend upon our feelings, or the goodness of the priest, or the size of the congregation. His presence is guaranteed by his promise, and sharing in the Eucharist must never be thought of as merely going to church, as for a school's founder's day service, or a sacred concert, or Remembrance Sunday and so on.

In the Eucharist you are one of millions, seen and unseen, who are keeping an appointment with Jesus. In the Eucharist we are in his presence. It is about him that we are thinking, so we speak and move with a reverence which we would not normally show in the bustle of the supermarket or in the office or factory.

In a few moments, you will be receiving Holy Communion for the first time. As you wait at the altar for the priest to reach you, speak to Jesus in your heart and say:

Come to my heart, Lord Jesus,
There is room in my heart for you.

And from now on make that your prayer every time you receive the sacrament.

Next, there is *prayer*. Christians are normal people, and we do all the things normal people do. We go shopping, ride on buses and trains, laugh and cry. Some misguided Christians even support England when they are playing the West Indies at cricket! But there is one activity which distinguishes Christians from many other people, and is a feature of life in Christ. Christians *pray*.

There are two good reasons for a Christian to do anything. Either because Christ did it and we are following his example, or because Christ asked us to do it and we are following his command. Both apply to prayer. Christ prayed a lot, and he taught and encouraged his friends to pray.

To pray is to be with God—to listen to him and speak to him. If you were to have an personal appointment with the Queen you would do your utmost to keep it and not to be late. You would pay attention to what she said to you and treasure it. You would express your pleasure at being in her company and thank her for inviting you. You might even go on to ask her help for some cause in which you are interested.

In prayer, you are in an even greater presence. So always begin with thanks to God for his goodness and generosity. Remember to apologize for wrongdoing, and ask his help for those whose needs are even greater than your own.

No one can be regularly in God's presence in prayer and not have his or her life transformed. Treat prayer seriously, and you will find yourself looking forward to being with God. Never hesitate to call on your parish priest for help with prayer.

So after this service, in which you have publicly committed yourself to Christ and received the gift of his Holy Spirit in confirmation, I want you to take your prayer book or Bible, and on the inside of the front cover write:

> Let your bearing towards one another arise out of your life in Christ Jesus.
>
> Philippians 2:5

Then write these four words:

BIBLE *EUCHARIST* *FELLOWSHIP* *PRAYER*

God bless and sustain you by his love in the life to which he has called you this day.

17

A WEDDING

Sermon preached at the wedding of Colin Richards and Christine Ball in Brownhill Road Baptist Church, 5 August 1978

Dear Colin and Christine,

Instead of preaching a sermon to you on your wedding day, I feel I would like to write you a personal letter, expressing some of the thoughts that have come into my mind, as during the past few weeks I have talked about you in prayer to God, and have talked with you about your wedding today and your marriage, which will follow from your wedding and which will continue all your life.

I would first of all like to say how thankful to God I am to have the privilege of sharing in your happiness on this occasion, and to thank you for your kindness in inviting me. As a clergyman I have dealings with many people at special points in their lives—sometimes at the peak of their happiness; sometimes in the depth of their despair; sometimes they are total strangers to me; and sometimes they are so well known to me that their hurt is my hurt, their joy is my joy.

And because the moments of sadness seem to be far more numerous than the moments of joy, I know you will forgive me when I say that I shall savour and treasure this particular moment of happiness with you all my life long. For already I feel part of your family, not merely because of my knowledge and respect for your parents, and my enjoyment of their hospitality, but because I genuinely feel that you have been led by God to find each other, and so for as long as you wish it, God will be with you.

That is why I would ask you to memorize this single verse of Scripture, taken from St Paul's letter to the Philippians, chapter 4 verse 19 (AV).

> My God shall supply all your need according to his riches in glory by Christ Jesus.

Let me tell you a story about another wedding, over nineteen hundred years ago in a little village in Galilee, called Cana. It was a happy occasion, and there had been so many toasts drunk to so many people—bride and groom, bride's parents, bridegroom's parents, guests, bridesmaids and so on—that the wine ran out.

One of the people invited to the wedding reception was a young religious teacher, but it was not the job of religious teachers to provide wine for wedding guests, so no one thought of him. No one except his mother, and she said to the servants: 'Do whatever he tells you.' So when later this teacher told the servants to fill the water pots with water and pass it to the Master of Ceremonies they did so, and lo and behold it was exactly what was needed. Wine!

Now I know you recognize that story. The teacher was Jesus, and Jesus is God in human form. God has the power and the will to provide you with whatever you need to live a life of perfect happiness in him. What is more, he has promised that he will do it. He knows what your real needs are, and should it happen that your wants differ from your needs it is your needs that he will be concerned with—because as human beings our knowledge is partial and sometimes we want things which are not for our good.

I do not want to bore you by going over all the things we have discussed in our sessions together. I know you will remember how I stressed that you will not find the word 'or' in the marriage service. It is always 'and'. For better, for worse, for richer for poorer, in sickness *and* in health; in prosperity *and* adversity. This is because your life together will include both happiness and unhappiness—indeed it is the experience of happiness which makes unhappiness bearable, and it is unhappiness which makes us appreciative of happiness.

You will remember, too, that it is not a case of each of you protecting yourself against losing any part of your individual life which you had before your wedding, but instead each of you will lose a bit, the better to fit together and become one. Even with machinery, no matter how precision-made it is, when moving parts are brought together they rub together a little before they settle into the perfect rhythm which is intended. But because the parts are made for one another, they will fit.

You will remember how I stressed that in choosing a wedding in church you have voluntarily chosen to make *your* marriage a marriage with three partners—God and yourselves. In such a partnership God will be consulted about decisions and directions, and he is by far the most knowledgeable of the three of you.

And through God you will be reminded that you do not live your lives in a small selfish world of your own, but he has given you the many gifts of good health, calm temperament, supportive parents, and above all love for one another, in order that you may be better able to love in the way that he loves you and to grow in this love, not by excluding other people but by including them. You have only to follow the advice which the mother of Jesus gave to the servants that day in Cana—advice which I want to give you: 'Whatever God tells you to do, do it.'

Finally, my dear Colin, my dear Christine, I pass on to you a little verse, which although it may sound soppy and sentimental, nevertheless conveys a profound truth. Here it is.

God has not promised skies always blue,
Flower-strewn pathways all your life through.
God has not promised sun without rain,
Joy without sorrow or peace without pain.

But God has promised strength for the day;
Rest for the labour, light for the way.

Grace for the trials, help from above,
Unfailing sympathy; undying love.

'My God shall supply all your need according to his riches in glory by Christ Jesus.' God bless you today and, in your life together, always.

Yours sincerely,
Wilfred Wood

18

THE GENTLE REVOLUTIONARY

Sermon preached at the Institution of The Reverend Andrew Studdart-Kennedy at St Oswald, Norbury, 2 February 1994

On the eighth day, when it was time to circumcise him, he was named Jesus, the name the angel had given him before he had been conceived.

When the time of their purification according to the Law of Moses had been completed, Joseph and Mary took him to Jerusalem to present him to the Lord (as it is written in the Law of the Lord, 'Every firstborn male is to be consecrated to the Lord'), and to offer a sacrifice in keeping with what is said in the Law of the Lord: 'a pair of doves or two young pigeons'.

Now there was a man in Jerusalem called Simeon, who was righteous and devout. He was waiting for the consolation of Israel, and the Holy Spirit was upon him. It had been revealed to him by the Holy Spirit that he would not die before he had seen the Lord's Christ. Moved by the Spirit, he went into the temple courts. When the parents brought in the child Jesus to do for him what the custom of the Law required, Simeon took him in his arms and praised God, saying:

'Sovereign Lord, as you have promised,
you now dismiss your servant in peace.

For my eyes have seen your salvation,
which you have prepared in the sight of all people,
a light for revelation to the Gentiles
and for glory to your people Israel.'

The child's father and mother marvelled at what was said about him. Then Simeon blessed them and said to Mary, his mother: 'This child is destined to cause the falling and rising of many...'

Luke 2:21–34 (NIV)

Today being 2 February, the Church celebrates, as it does on this date every year, the Presentation of Christ. According to religious custom at the time, every first-born son, within a certain time after his birth, had to be taken to the temple along with a symbolic gift. This is what Joseph and Mary were doing for the baby Jesus, no doubt along with many other parents, when the old man Simeon spotted them. He came over, took the baby in his arms and blessed him.

Then he said a strange thing. He said: 'This child is destined to cause the falling and rising of many...' It must have seemed a very strange prophecy at the time, because not only was Jesus born into a nation that was then a subject-nation ruled by the powerful Roman conquerors, but he was born into a *poor* family, as evidenced by the fact that the gift consisted of two pigeons—a concession made to those who could not afford a lamb.

Everything about the child suggested weakness and poverty, yet even then Simeon could see that he was to be an agent of change and revolution—that through him some who were mighty would be brought down, and some who were humble would be lifted up.

We know now how accurate was that prophecy. Jesus grew up to be poor—as the world sees poverty. So far as we know he followed the humble trade of a carpenter before leaving that to become a travelling preacher. He never owned a home, held any office, wrote any books, commanded any soldiers, erected any buildings. He was also weak as the world sees weakness—because when it suited the authorities they were able to seize him, pretend to give him a proper trial, and kill him.

Yet Simeon proved to be right. For this gentle revolutionary was armed with an honesty and faith in God so strong that his message of God's love for all turned the world upside down. Why?

Because he changed people's thinking about themselves. Lepers, beggars, prostitutes, Samaritans, all of whom had been labelled 'sinners' by those who made the rules, discovered that they were really lovely people because

God loved them, and with this discovery they could stand ten feet tall! The pompous, the powerful, whose wealth and status assured them of the favours of dishonest bureaucrats and of religious respectability from servile and time-serving priests, found that in his presence these things were no more substantial than were the Emperor's new clothes. They too were being invited to change their thinking about themselves. Sadly, many of them chose not to. They fell.

We ought not therefore to be surprised to find that whenever the Church, as the embodiment of the spirit of this unlikely revolutionary, has been true to him, it has been an agent of change and therefore a threat to those who, in the status quo, possess the world's power and respectability. Small wonder that they, the world's rulers, have employed time-serving apologists and so-called theologians to distort the teachings of Christ and present him instead as a defender of the status quo.

For example, in times past, those who enjoyed playing at war could convince themselves that they were on God's side, and name their murderous assaults on other nations 'religious crusades'. Those who made slaves of other human beings and treated them as disposable property could disguise it as benevolently taking civilization to savages.

Yet even in the darkest hours God raised up unlikely gentle revolutionaries in surprising situations. Such as an army padre on the bloody battlefields of the First World War. A young white monk in the black shanty towns of South Africa. A Baptist preacher in the segregation of the American Deep South. A Catholic bishop shot down on the steps of his cathedral in Central America.

In all these cases their call for justice was made in the name of the Jesus who wants things changed. They knew, as Christ knew, that the Church is a community of first-born sons, where everyone, male and female, Jew and gentile, black and white, is equally and uniquely loved. And for as long as the world and its rulers reject such a call for justice, so long will the Church be destined for their falling and rising.

So here in our country at this time, when almost daily we are battered with new revelations of misbehaviour in high places; of disreputable deals to sell more and more guns and bombs to people who should be buying food; of public servants being economical with the truth and when around us are the signs of social disintegration, we are thankful that God continues to lay his hands on young men and women for the purpose of building up his church for witness in the world of today and tomorrow.

Before he formed these young men and women in the womb he knew them. He loves them with an everlasting love and, after the pattern of his son Jesus, has destined them to cause the rising and falling of many in our time. I am pleased that in recent months I have had the privilege of instituting a number of such young men of great promise, including some here in Croydon North deanery.

Doubtless when we speak like this there are those who retort, 'Physician, heal thyself' and point to differences and disagreements in the Church, notably over the ordination of women as priests. I remember a few years ago on a visit to the Council of European Churches in Geneva, in the immediate aftermath of the break-up of the Soviet Republic, hearing how in these former communist countries, at every level, city, town and village, Christian leaders were in great demand to chair meetings. Why? Because church leaders were the only people in the community with any experience of chairing meetings where there was a difference of opinion and no single party line!

It may be that in a world where nations and tribes possess the military capability to destroy themselves and the world, what is needed is *a model of living with differences*. If the Church in general, and Christians in particular, can demonstrate that among us the greatest political, ideological and even theological differences are subject to the overriding law of love and mutual respect, the Church itself may be that model.

So our worship this evening is an occasion of great joy and excitement. It is a kind of wedding really. Andrew and Annie are joining the faithful here at St Oswald's to begin a new life together in the community. Andrew is not being made Vicar of St Oswald's *Church*, but Vicar of the Parish of St Oswald's. That is to say, his concern must not be for Church members only but, together with the Church members, to care for the whole community within the boundaries of this parish. Together you will remember that the Church is a society that exists for those who are not its members, and that loving service of such a community will require you to work alongside (though not uncritically) other caring agencies, some voluntary, some statutory.

You are not alone, and in addition to the resources of friendship and support which you will find in your deanery colleagues and ecumenical partners, you have the interparochial ministries of our diocese such as lay training, education and youthwork, race relations, and local ministry development—to mention only a few—who are there to support the work and ministry in our parishes. Please do not hesitate to call on them, because wheels do not have to be invented every day!

You first priority must of course be worship. It is in Word and Sacrament that your common life will be fed and strengthened. It is a duty that is a joy, and those who join you in worship for the first time should feel not only that they are welcome but that they were expected. If in your worship there is reverence and awe, and a quiet enjoyment of Christ's presence among you, Christ will be encountered, and there will be, please God, more rising than falling. God bless you in your pilgrimage together.

19

RETIREMENT

Sermon preached at the service of thanksgiving to mark the retirement of Mrs Thelma Thomas, St Cuthbert's, Palmer's Green, 28 December 1990

> Put on then, as God's chosen ones, holy and beloved, compassion, kindness, lowliness, meekness, and patience, forbearing one another and, if one has a complaint against another, forgiving each other; as the Lord has forgiven you, so you also must forgive. And above all these put on love, which binds everything together in perfect harmony. And let the peace of Christ rule in your hearts, to which indeed you were called in the one body. And be thankful. Let the word of Christ dwell in you richly, teach and admonish one another in all wisdom, and sing psalms and hymns and spiritual songs with thankfulness in your hearts to God. And whatever you do, in word or deed, do everything in the name of the Lord Jesus, giving thanks to God the Father through him.
>
> Colossians 3:12–17 (RSV)

> On the way to Jerusalem [Jesus] was passing along between Samaria and Galilee. And as he entered a village, he was met by ten lepers, who stood at a distance and lifted up their voices and said, 'Jesus, Master, have mercy on us.' When he saw them he said to them, 'Go and show yourselves to the priests.' And as they went they were cleansed. Then one of them, when he saw that he was healed, turned back, praising God with a loud voice; and he fell on his face at Jesus' feet, giving him thanks. Now he was a Samaritan. Then said Jesus, 'Were not ten cleansed? Where are the nine? Was no one found to return and give praise to God except this foreigner?' And he said to him, 'Rise and go your way; your faith has made you well.'
>
> Luke 17:11–19 (RSV)

In the infant school's nativity play the first of the three kings approached the manger, bowed, presented his gift: 'Gold', he said, and withdrew. The second king approached the manger, bowed and presented his gift: 'Myrrh', he said, and withdrew. The third king approached, bowed and presented his gift: 'Frank sent this', he said.

The little chap may not have got the word right, but he had got the idea right. He realized that what he had was really a gift from someone else.

This is the great distinguishing mark of Christian people. Christians living in a society are affected in the same way as non-Christians by all that goes on around them. Rain and snow fall on Christians and non-Christians alike; bereavement, sickness, accidents happen to us all, and there can also be prosperity and happiness. But where the non-Christian sees adversity as his bad luck, and sees himself as a self-made man whose prosperity is the result of his own cleverness or hard work, the Christian sees all these things as a gift from God. That is why the Christian is not envious of other people's prosperity or good fortune—he or she is just thankful for what God gives. So a thankful heart is the basis of Christian living. There is a lot of truth in the song we sometimes sing, which goes like this:

When upon life's billows you are tempest-tossed,
When you are discouraged, thinking all is lost,
Count your many blessings, name them one by one
And it will surprise you what the Lord has done.

A former Bishop of Southwark, Mervyn Stockwood, used to say that God has been so good to us that we should count our blessings, not one by one but ton by ton!

This is also the part which the Church must play in the life of the nation. In the story of the ten lepers which we have just heard read, all ten lepers were cleansed, but only one returned to thank God for the gift of health. All humankind is God's family and all humankind receive God's gifts. But the Church is that part of God's family that knows it is part of God's family, so that in worship and praise the Church thanks God, not only on its own behalf, but also on behalf of all those other people who receive God's gifts, but are too busy or indifferent to thank God themselves.

It is also interesting that the one leper who came back to thank Jesus was a Samaritan, a foreigner. So often people are puzzled by the joy and exuberance which characterize West Indians at worship, because they know something of the difficulties which many West Indians experience in their lives. What they do not appreciate is the deep sense of thankfulness to

God which upholds us West Indians in our faith. Each one of us knows that at the very moment we were born, at the very same minute of the same day of the same week of the same month of the same year, there were thousands of other babies born around the world, and that even today, in every 48 hours, 46,000 of such children die before the age of five because of starvation, malnutrition and related diseases. It is not because of anything *we* have done ourselves that we have survived while others have not. So we are thankful to God. And if ever we are tempted to complain because we have no *shoes*, we remember that there are people who have no *feet*. And we thank God.

So it is right that for the Christian, every milestone in this earthly pilgrimage—birth, baptism, marriage, childbirth, employment, retirement, and even death—should be marked by thanksgiving. And I am very pleased to be sharing in this service to mark the retirement of someone who has always been a better Christian than I have been.

It is a long time now since my big sister used to drag me unwillingly to church twice every Sunday in the hot sun, first to morning service, and then to Sunday school in the afternoon. Later, when I was an impecunious student in theological college in Barbados, and everybody thought God's angels dressed in white, had wings and carried harps, I knew that they wore a postman's uniform, and brought me postal orders from my sister who was a nurse in England! And she has never given up looking after me!

I can still recall the scene in St Paul's Cathedral, London, on 21 December, 1962, more than 28 years ago when I was ordained, when the only other black person in the Cathedral was my sister, heavily pregnant, at the end of the queue, going up to make her communion. So it was very good in the same Cathedral twenty-three years later, when the scene was very different, and I was back there again, this time to be consecrated a bishop in the Church of God, to hear her sniffling in the pew behind me! Her love, support, encouragement and prayers have all helped to make me what I am—so you see, she has a lot to answer for!

I also know that I am not the only person to recognize and thank God for her Christian virtues. Many years ago I was attending a training course at Haywards Heath in Sussex and was in conversation with one of the tutors. This tutor said to me: 'Of course, the West Indians I admire most are the district nurses. My mother, who is now dead, was nursed in her last days by a lovely West Indian district nurse. She was a real Christian, cheerful and efficient, and my mother grew to be very fond of her.' I said I was very pleased to hear this because my own sister was a district nurse.

Some days later I was at the same table as this tutor and overheard her telling someone that she lived in Tottenham. 'Isn't that in Harringey?' I asked, 'my sister is a district nurse in Harringey.' 'Is your sister Mrs Thomas? That is my mother's district nurse that I was telling you about!'

God's ways are truly wondrous. Only a few days ago I was on a visit to the Church in Zimbabwe. It was a most moving experience, because the congregations, having been told that the Bishop of Croydon, England, was coming, expected to see a white bishop and could scarcely contain themselves at the sight of a bishop from England who was as black as they were!

But the experience that will always live with me was a visit to the very humble home of an elderly retired priest who was too ill to get to the church. He made a moving speech in which he thanked God for all the blessings he had bestowed on him all his long life—his wife and children; his home and cattle; his job as a police instructor; his service in church as catechist and priest, and now, at the end of his life, to have two bishops under his roof, celebrating the service of Holy Communion in his home. God was just too good to him. He had long been ready to leave this life, but now he could hardly wait to thank God face to face!

That is the example I would like all of us present this evening to to take with us into 1991. In terms of this world's goods he was a poor man, and had been poor all his life. But a thankful heart had given him a peace and contentment that at the end of his earthly life he could look forward to life beyond the grave with pleasurable anticipation.

God grant that at every milestone in our own lives we will be able to say as Dag Hammarskjold: 'For all that has been—thanks: to all that shall be—Yes!'

20

GIVE GOD THE PRAISE!

Sermon preached at the consecration of Canon Herman Spence as the fifth Bishop of Kingston, Jamaica, on Saturday 11 November 1989.

I thank God for the privilege of bringing you greetings on this occasion from your fellow Christians in Britain, particularly those from Jamaica and other parts of the Caribbean, and those in the diocese of Southwark. My episcopal colleague, the Bishop of Kingston, England, is particularly disappointed not to be here since, like the Bishop-designate of Kingston, Jamaica whom he has met, he also is a graduate of the

Episcopal Divinity School in Boston. He sends his greetings and his love.

Let us pray. In the name of the living God, Father, Son and Holy Spirit. Come, Holy Spirit, and sanctify us, giving us thoughts that lead to prayer, prayer that leads to love, and love that leads to life in you forever. Amen.

'Give God the praise...'

John 9:24 (RSV)

On 22 October 1957, more than thirty-two years ago, a number of freshmen, including the present Bishop of St John's, Antigua, and at least two other priests in this congregation and myself, were formally admitted to Codrington College to train for the priesthood. The sermon then was preached by that wise, saintly and learned Gay Lisle Griffith Mandeville, who as Bishop of Barbados rejoiced in the title +Gay Barbados.

He preached on the nature of God's call to prophetic ministry, service and leadership, and I particularly remember how he kept muttering throughout the sermon, almost as though speaking to himself, the Greek words: '*Klytos pathein, klytos pathein*'—called to suffer. He was no masochist, and he was not extolling suffering for its own sake. Rather he was reminding us of this peculiar feature of a call from God.

He reminded us of Joseph, who was sold into slavery by his brothers and as a result was able to save their lives; of Moses, who had to hide in the wilderness for fear of betrayal by his own people, and there was called by God to lead them out of slavery to freedom in the Promised Land. He reminded us of Jesus Christ himself, whose task of rescuing humankind from the slavery of sin involved his suffering and his death.

The Bishop chose to remind us of this just at the moment when we were surrounded by friends and admirers who wished us well and shared our own conviction that we would be doing great things for God and his people. His words are just as appropriate today in the joy and pageantry of this splendid occasion as they were so many years ago. Called to suffer. It is God who calls—give God the praise.

There is another feature of God's call which should not escape us. A call from God is never a reward for anything that we are or anything we have done. God is always more interested in what a man or woman can become than in what he or she has been.

In 1 Corinthians 1:26–27 (AV) St Paul puts it like this:

> For ye see your calling, brethren, how that not many wise men after the flesh, not many mighty, not many noble, are called: But God

> hath chosen the foolish things of the world to confound the wise; and God hath chosen the weak things of the world to confound the things which are mighty...

'Give God the praise!'

I first met Herman Spence soon after we were both made deacons, almost twenty-eight years ago. It was my first visit to Jamaica, on my way to England, and he and Ewart Gordon and Peter Mullings showed me around Kingston. Our friendship was cemented somewhat when later, in England, I prepared June, his wife-to-be, for her confirmation. We have kept in touch and remained firm friends ever since, and my respect and admiration and affection for him as priest, friend and brother have grown and grown. So I know him to be a man of prayer, for whom liturgy and worship centred on regular celebration of the Eucharist are as vital as fresh air. My own ministry has been supported by his prayers, and by the friendship and hospitality which he, his wife June and their children, Christopher, Simone and Nicole, have extended to me. It is for me, therefore, the greatest privilege to be invited to take part in this service.

There are those who have known Herman from childhood who will testify that for as far back as they can remember he has wanted nothing else but to be a priest. He grew up in a deeply religious family and the good wishes and prayers of many helped him on his way. Some of these have passed from life to life, such as his own parents, his sisters Enid and Gladys, schoolteacher, Miss Gunning, parish priest Canon Cope and Bishop Cyril Swaby. But there are others happily still with us, including his own ten brothers and sisters, Aunt Milly Davis, Uncle Ted Hezekiah and teacher Mrs Prescod, and Bishop Tommy Clarke, who rejoice to see this day.

Then there are those who in his more than twenty-six years as curate and Rector of St Andrew's, Halfway Tree, have had good cause to thank God for him and his ministry. His faithful stewardship of word and sacrament, his pastoral care in times of personal crises, bereavements and anxieties; his teaching of the faith of Christ's holy, catholic and apostolic Church which has equipped them for witness in their daily lives; his readiness to laugh with them, to cry with them, always to love them as God's precious children entrusted to his care, mean that understandably many are bitterly disappointed that limitations of space prevent them from adding their voices to ours in this church today even as they join their prayers with ours. Herman is very special to them.

And there are those of his fellow priests and members of Synod whose recognition of his qualities was expressed by their accepting the Diocesan

Bishop's invitation to elect him Bishop Suffragan of Kingston.

Yet it is for none of these reasons, worthy as they may be, that Herman is to become a bishop. It is for one reason, and one reason only. That God looked on him and loved him and wanted him to be a bishop—and has seen to it that he becomes one. Give God the praise!

'Give God the praise' has a significant double meaning where it occurs in John 9:24. In addition to its obvious meaning, it was also a colloquial phrase meaning, 'Tell the truth!' It was festival time in Jerusalem, and the religious establishment had made it known that anyone suggesting that Jesus was the Christ should be thrown out of the synagogue. There was a man who had been blind from birth, and Jesus had anointed his eyes and sent him to wash in the pool of Siloam. He did this and was able to see.

The authorities questioned him and his parents, refusing to believe his story, and badgering him instead with, 'Give God the praise,' meaning, 'Tell the truth.' But the man refused to lie in order to save the face of the religious authorities. He refused to deny the truth of his experience in order to accommodate the conventional wisdom of the status quo or to please those with power. So 'Give God the praise' is not a bad motto for a bishop in the Church of God today.

'The Church', wrote the late Archbishop Michael Ramsey, 'lives towards God and the world. Towards God it worships; towards the world it preaches the Gospel, it brings people into fellowship with God, it infects the world with righteousness; it speaks of divine principles on which the life of humanity is ordered.'

The Church is like nothing else on earth and like nothing else that the world has ever known. For what nation or empire or tribe has there ever been whose supreme motivation in all things and at all times is meant to be love? This is the Church in which bishops share a special responsibility to further its unity, uphold its discipline, guard its faith and promote its mission throughout the world, doing this by speaking in the name of God and interpreting the Gospel of Christ. An awesome responsibility!

For these responsibilities have a built-in tension where 'upholding discipline' and 'guarding faith' can appear to conflict with promoting mission.

The bishops will share with all their people a firm belief in the changelessness of God and of eternal truths. But they will also bear in mind William Temple's reminder that the Church exists primarily for those who are not its members. It has a mission to the world. They must resist every pressure to be spokesmen for a bygone age when allegedly men and women were more godly, when there was more good and less evil in the world. We all too easily forget that there was a time when authoritative religious teaching held that the sun moved around the earth (and not the other way around) and that even someone of the intellectual brilliance of St Augustine could state that slavery was due to the sinfulness of the slaves!

So in all the complex and perplexing questions of today's world—questions of justice and peace, of militarism, political oppression and persecution, economic exploitation, apartheid and racial discrimination, the ordination of women to the priesthood, human sexuality or the relationship between the Church in the Caribbean and the governments in the various territories, to name only a few—the bishops must guide the Church away from both an automatic acceptance of the status quo and an unthinking and simplistic embracing of every new prescription.

In making Christ known to every new generation, bishops must trust the Holy Spirit to guide them into truth, and have courage to proclaim that truth. If an action is theologically right, and morally right, how for the Church can it be politically wrong? The abolition of slavery would have been delayed for ever if it had been dependent on all the theologians agreeing that black people had souls! And the one thing that all the Church leaders in Birmingham, Alabama could agree on was that the time was not ripe for what Martin Luther King was trying to do!

Because God continues to make all things new, bishops must work with others to usher Church and society forward, communicating a sense of urgency without impatience, pomposity or arrogance. Nothing, nothing is more unseemly in this Church founded by a naked, crucified, suffering Christ than a pompous bishop intoxicated with self-esteem and the power he wields because others see him as a representative of the God they serve. The soul of the bishop is no more valuable in the sight of God than the soul of the common prostitute. They are both of infinite worth. Give God the praise!

And now Herman, my friend and brother, all these solemn things said, I am going to presume upon our friendship to address you directly.

The task to which you have been called is a heavy one, and you cannot do it in your own strength. Just before I left Croydon to come to Jamaica I was speaking to a wise and holy woman, herself no stranger to the pain and pleasure of vocation. I asked her: 'What should I say to a man about to be consecrated bishop?' Knowing her sense of humour I was expecting her to say something like, 'Tell him not to bother—we have too many bishops already!'

Instead, she answered in serious vein. 'Tell him,' she said, 'that if he thinks that up to now he has known loneliness, it is nothing to what he will experience. But he is not to worry. Christ has been there before him.'

This echoes some advice given me many years ago in Barbados when I stopped on my bicycle to exchange greetings with a man forking a piece of land. 'So I hear you are going in for the ministry,' he said. 'What does that mean?' 'It means,' I said, 'that I will spend four years in Codrington College, and if at the end of that time God is still with me I will be ordained.' 'Oh no,' said this earthy man, 'God will always be there—it is if you remain with him!'

My brother, you will never be alone in the cause of right. The invisible heavenly host which even now rejoice with us as you are elevated on the prayers of the faithful, will always be there, and always in every tribulation you will hear our Master's voice: 'Be of good cheer. I have overcome the world.'

So first I want to urge you—retain your sense of humour. Laugh often and heartily—with the laughter of a man who enjoys people, with all their quirks and eccentricities, knowing them to be God's handiwork and loving them because they are. And laugh at yourself sometimes. Your courtesy, dignity and integrity have all grown through exercise. Sadly, your physical frame has stubbornly refused any such encouragement! You will be able to do this if you maintain a proper sense of detachment from earthly notions of success and failure.

But detachment is not the same as ignorance. I remember that some years ago some of our West Indian cricketers let us all down rather badly by going to play cricket in South Africa. On their return a reporter asked one of them what he thought of Nelson Mandela. 'Mandela?' he mused thoughtfully, 'let me see. I don't think he played against us!'

Next, do your best to strengthen and encourage your brethren—the priests to whom you must now be father-in-God. I commend to you a practice which is increasingly being adopted in other places—that of an annual ministerial interview. So every priest will know that at least once a year he will be able to spend some time with his bishop—not because there is a crisis, or to talk about parish finances, but because his bishop is concerned to share with him the joys and sorrows of ministry, the matters that give him encouragement and those that cause him concern, and to counsel and advise when this is helpful. He will know that he and his bishop are fellow pilgrims, struggling together to be faithful shepherds of Christ's flock. It would be wonderful if every one of your clergy could think of you as a friend.

Thirdly, continue to treasure your wife and children. Vocations to marriage and parenthood are not lesser vocations. They too come from God. It is inconceivable that it should be his will that a call to the priesthood or episcopate should destroy his other calls. The peculiar temptations of the priest's calling which make him the centre of other people's interests, which give him the last word in many discussions, and a high profile in social and community activity, are multiplied many times in the case of a bishop. This most assuredly will make him a stranger to those nearest to him unless there is adequate time for relaxation and recreation which involves them, and in which they have a genuine role in decision-making. Herman, my friend, you are much blessed in June, Christopher, Simone and Nicole. Continue to enjoy them, and enable them to enjoy you.

Finally, my brother, enjoy being a bishop, enjoy being Herman Spence. Be full of love for all—admirers and detractors alike, and always act on the advice St Paul the Apostle gave to his young disciple Timothy:

> Stir into flame the gift that God gave you in the laying-on of my hands. For God has not given us the spirit of fear, but of strength and of love, and of a sound mind.
>
> 2 Timothy 1:6–7

The gift of God's Spirit is yours—there is no need to fear. Give God the praise!

And now to God the Father, Son and Holy Spirit, be honour and glory, thanksgiving and praise, for ever and ever. Amen.

21

ELAINE WESTOW

A eulogy given at the funeral of Elaine Westow at the Roman Catholic Church of St Osmond in Salisbury on 25 January 1993

It is neither modesty—false or real—nor a polite disclaimer when I say that I am woefully inadequate for the privilege and responsibility of putting into words what has brought so many of us here today: the admiration, the respect, the affection and, above all, the love we have for Elaine. At the same time it is strangely comforting to know that although doubtless there are others whose efforts might be better than mine, there is no one on earth and no words in any language that could do justice to the total Elaine.

The all-loving, self-giving, other-affirming, sensitive and caring Elaine; the enthusiastic, energetic Elaine of the bear-hug and infectious laughter, the embodiment of those great theological virtues of Faith, Hope and Love. Elaine—and Theo—are at the centre of a spider's web of friendship which must reach nearly every part of the world.

It was some twenty-seven years ago that I first met Theo, when I presented a paper at a Downside Symposium and accepted his invitation to visit him and Elaine here in Salisbury. We became firm friends immediately, and some time later, when my wife and I married, they invited us to spend our honeymoon in their house while they were on holiday in Africa—an invitation we readily accepted.

Since then, I have had more cups of tea, more meals and more drinks at their house than I can count. It was a necessary stop whenever I was within reach of it. Theo and Elaine have stayed with us in London. Together we have walked on a Christian CND march to Canterbury. Together we have danced at the West Indian carnival in Notting Hill. Invariably the friends to whom I introduced this remarkable couple were impressed by them and in turn became their friends.

Those from overseas would always enquire about them. Elaine's wide interests and sympathies—travel, books, education, politics, music and art to mention only a few—meant that people, especially young people, were instantly at home with her and they opened themselves to her warmth.

How Elaine enjoyed people—with all their fads and idiosyncrasies! She accepted them as God's handiwork and loved them because they are.

Elaine was a teacher and a rather special one. Education is more than schooling or teaching or training. Rather, it is the drawing out of inherent gifts and the development and flourishing of these gifts. In this sense Elaine was no mere teacher but a natural educator, and her contribution to the schools in which she worked—notably the South Wiltshire Grammar School for Girls—is not to be measured by the posts or titles she held, but by her influence for good on the lives of so many of their pupils. So many can testify to the part she played in their finding a sense of purpose and direction in their lives; in helping them to the confident knowledge that they were loved for themselves, not merely for what they represented, and that in every way they had a beauty other than what was in the eye of the beholder.

Elaine and Theo shared a deep sense of the oneness of the human race as one family under God. For them every human being is entitled to the freedom to live as God intends, and we should all be concerned to see that this is so. For the individual this requires our love; for groups it requires justice.

These are sentiments most right-thinking people will echo, but Elaine was essentially a practical person, so for her this meant *action*. Hence her dedication to the work of the United Nations Association. Hence her devoted work with the local Samaritans. Hence her support for Amnesty International and Prisoners of Conscience. Hence her membership of CND, Aldermaston and other marches, and visits to Greenham Common. Hence her membership of the Labour Party and her services on the Magistrates' bench. Hence her work with ecumenical and inter-faith groups. Hence her support for work on the justice and peace issues such as third world debt and racism, and her championing the cause of marginalized and persecuted groups in our society such as gypsies and gay folk.

For these causes, all dear to her heart, there was never a fund-raising jumble sale too many; never a protest meeting too many. Time would always be found for delivering leaflets, first by bicycle, and when that was no longer practicable, on foot and by bus.

Many have witnessed her good-humoured confrontations with those in authority when their exercise of power lacked compassion. She was an indefatigable letter writer—not only to the Press on public issues, but to her many friends in this country and overseas. Certainly for me the sight of that beautiful handwriting on an envelope was always a most welcome one. I suppose now in heaven she will know how effective or not her letter writing has been. I know that in her impatience years ago she did write to the Archbishop of Canterbury asking when was he going to make Wilfred Wood a bishop!

I have left until now the two loves of Elaine's life which were the twin pillars on which her life's work was built—her devotion to her husband, Theo, and her devotion to the Christian faith fed by word and sacrament in membership of the Catholic Church.

Theo is a beautiful person and it is not surprising that Elaine fell in love with him. He sees nothing but good in everyone and his gentle manner belies the passion of his indignation in the face of injustice. If he had a sense of frustration it is that the gifts with which he is endowed for scholarly creative writing, which could free the spirit and liberate the mind, have seemed to count for so little in a world where the acquisitive instinct and the sheer brute force of international capitalism and nuclear weaponry reigned supreme.

He needed Elaine's no-nonsense activism just as she needed his penetrating analysis of changing situations and passing fancies, and always they were there for each other. Love is not giving; love is not receiving—love is giving *and* receiving, a human reflection of the relationship between the Persons of the Blessed Trinity. Theo and Elaine have been, were and are, very much in love.

It would be presumptuous of me to dwell too much on Elaine's love for and membership of the Catholic Church, or to attempt to add to what Father Thomas said in his sermon. But we Christians can name the source of that strength which is made perfect in weakness. St Paul in the sixth chapter of his second letter to the Corinthians was not thinking of Elaine Westow. But he described her perfectly when he wrote:

> We recommend ourselves by the innocence of our behaviour, our grasp of truth, our patience and kindliness; by gifts of the Holy Spirit, by sincere love, by declaring the truth, by the power of God. We wield the weapons of righteousness in right hand and left. Honour and dishonour, praise and blame, are alike our lot: we are impostors who speak the truth, the unknown men whom all men know; dying we still live on; disciplined by suffering, we are not done to death; in our sorrows we have always cause for joy; poor ourselves, we bring wealth to many; penniless, we own the world.
>
> 2 Corinthians 6:6–10 (NEB)

That source is Jesus Christ—suffering, crucified, risen, ascended, glorified. Elaine knew and loved the Lord Jesus above everyone and everything else.

I like to think that Elaine, whose Catholicism embraced without condescension Anglicans, Methodists, Baptists, Quakers and everyone who loved the Lord Jesus, is thrilled at the representative character of this congregation. Because I know that in God's mercy she has passed from life to life, I will always think of her as a candle. For two reasons.

First because of that beautiful saying: 'It is better to light a small candle than merely curse the darkness'—and this is precisely what she did by her active expression of her Christian faith. Certainly for people like me individuals like her were tiny points of hope in the dark days of Powellism.

Secondly, there are those joke candles which look just like other candles, but whenever you blow them out they burst into flame again. In death as in life, saints like Elaine are a flame which will never be put out and will always light the path of others. In God's mercy, may she rest in Christ, and rise with him in glory.

Section Three:

Community

22

CIVIC SERVICE

Sermon preached at the Civic Service in St Stephen's (City) Church, Bristol, 24 March 1991

> God has shown you, O man, what is good. And what does the Lord require of you, but to do justly and love mercy, and to walk humbly with your God.
>
> Micah 6:8

When we refer to a person or thing as being good we have the idea of success or efficiency in mind. So a good doctor is an efficient doctor, and we can even call a man a good crook—if we think he is successful in his dishonesty! And we can use the word 'good' as a degree of comparison, which may be exceeded by 'better' and 'best'.

But this is not the biblical usage of the word 'good'. In the Bible 'good' denotes perfection which cannot be surpassed. So when on the Mount of Transfiguration Peter says, 'Lord, it is good for us to be here,' he is saying that there is nothing better than to be with Jesus in glory. Similarly, when a Jewish leader addressed Jesus as 'Good master', Jesus replied: 'Why do you call me good? Only God is good!' In other words, 'Are you acknowledging me as God?'

These words from the prophecy of Micah were written some seven hundred years before the birth of Christ, and it is worth noting that, even as early as that, men and women had come to the knowledge that their true good, their perfection, lay in the performance of God's will and the fulfilment of his requirements.

These requirements are twofold, involving duty towards God—which is to walk humbly with God—and duty towards their fellows—which is to do justly and love mercy.

Many years later Jesus himself was to repeat this injunction with even greater emphasis. He said, 'You shall *love* the Lord your God with all your heart, with all your mind and with all your strength, and your neighbour as yourself.'

This then is what is good or perfect for humankind. Duty towards God and duty towards our fellows—a duty that is rooted in love.

But the history of the world shows that humankind has often found this double obligation too great a demand, and has responded by trying to do the one while neglecting the other. Sometimes we have tried to do our duty towards God without due regard towards our fellows. In the past and the present, people have acted in ways which are totally contradictory.

On the one hand, there has been much religious observance, such as crowded churches, loud and long prayers. On the other hand, there have been many unjust and immoral social conditions. People seemed unable to see the bizarre inconsistency of one Christian burning another to death in the name of God. Neither could they see the contradiction in a pious, churchgoing Christian getting rich from the slave trade or from the labours of half-starved, underpaid workers—including children working many hours a day in appalling conditions.

The ringing words of Bishop Frank Weston when he addressed the Anglo-Catholic Congress of 1923 in the Albert Hall in London were both a rebuke and an inspiration:

But I say to you, and I say it with all the earnestness that I have... You cannot worship Jesus in the Sacrament, and Jesus on the throne of glory, when you are sweating Him in the bodies and souls of His children. You have your Mass, you have your altars; you have begun to get your tabernacles.

Now go out into the highways and hedges, and look for Jesus in the ragged and the naked; in the oppressed and the sweated, in those who have lost hope, and those who are struggling to make good.

Look for Jesus in them*—and when you have found Him, gird yourself with His towel of fellowship and wash His feet, in the persons of His brethren.*

But sometimes humankind has tried to do right by its neighbours while denying God any place in the scheme of things. This has led to various materialistic ideologies, of which the best-known example is Communism. But when you educate men and women without religion you only make them clever devils, as the existence and brutalities of such people as Stalin have shown. It is right that we should be properly clothed and fed. But we human beings have souls—and our souls know a hunger that can only be satisfied by God.

Where does government, central or local, come in all this? In the Gospels some questioners tried to trap Jesus by asking if it was right to pay taxes to Caesar, the Roman emperor. After pointing out that the coins were Caesar's coins, and had the image of Caesar engraved on them, Jesus said: 'Pay Caesar what is due to Caesar, and to God what is due to God' (Matthew 22:21).

Many of us have heard politicians (upset by comments from Church leaders) use this saying to suggest that politics and Christian witness ought to be kept in two separate compartments. I believe that is to misunderstand Our Lord's teaching, which is that Caesar could not be worshipped—only God should be worshipped—and that people have a duty to support order and government because anarchy is no part of God's plan for his world. But at the heart of Our Lord's command is the assumption that Caesar also will respect his proper limits and do his basic duties.

For it is a basic duty of government to make it as easy as possible to live as God intends. And it is irresponsible of any Christian to call on others to obey the laws of the land if he or she is not doing everything possible to ensure that such laws are in accordance with the laws of God.

The practice of politics is therefore a worthy vocation for Christians. It is also entirely appropriate that our representatives in local and central government should be chosen on the basis of one person, one vote. This is in keeping with a fundamental Christian precept, that every person is someone for whom Christ has died, and every soul is of unique value in the eyes of God.

We and our representatives should never lose sight of the value and importance of the individual. There will always be pressures to reduce people to statistics or units: to lump us together as though we were carbon copies of one another. It is a Christian duty to resist such pressures.

That is why those of us who espouse the creating in our country of a truly multi-ethnic, multi-cultural society do not want to see us all flattened into somebody's mythical idea of what an English person is supposed to be. What we seek instead is a society of equal opportunity—cultural diversity in an atmosphere of mutual appreciation.

That is also why we must deplore the increasing tendency in our consumer society to see human beings first and foremost as economic units. For example, if you listen to British Rail announcements at some railway stations, you will hear that you are no longer referred to as a 'traveller' or a 'passenger' but a 'customer'. The almost daily changes in tax systems, benefits calculations and the value of money also add to this climate, with the result that unless we are careful we shall acquire a casino mentality, in which the acquisition of money becomes the first purpose of our existence.

I wish we would stop talking about persons in the abstract, such as 'the unemployed' or 'the disabled' or 'blacks' or 'the homeless', because one feature of a person's existence can never describe the total person. Instead, we must think of unemployed *people*, of differently-abled *people*, of black *people* and of homeless *people*.

Nor must we think that democracy means control by the *majority* of the people. Rather, democracy means control by *all* the people—each sharing equally in privileges, duties and responsibilities. That is why, in a democracy, it is an essential duty to protect minorities, and why the greatness of a nation or a society must be measured, not by military might or economic power, but by its concern for its weakest and most vulnerable members.

I was a member of the Archbishop of Canterbury's Commission on Urban Priority Areas. We spent two years visiting cities and housing estates up and down the country, and we saw the conditions under which many people are struggling to retain some personal dignity and civil pride in the face of increasing deprivation.

Our report, *Faith in the City*, came out in 1985, and it only went a little way to alert those of us who lived in (what was then) the prosperous South to the alienating conditions of unemployment, debts and loss of dignity with which many of our fellow citizens (especially in the Midlands and in the North) were struggling day in and day out. At the time I was at a loss to know how this reality could be conveyed to comfortable people. Certainly television seemed to find no time for this in between episodes of *Dallas*, *Dynasty* and the like.

But since *Faith in the City* came out things have changed, and the recession has spread throughout Britain. People are discovering for themselves the distress of debts and unemployment—and this is happening in every class of society. But there is a new class appearing in our society which has ominous implications. In 1987 I attended the annual lecture of St George's House, Windsor, given by Professor Ralf Dahrendorf on the subject 'The Underclass and Britain's Future'.

It was chilling to hear him say (and he said it reluctantly and with regret) that in a critical sense the underclass is made up of people who are literally not needed, and that people who have no stake in the world in which they are living cannot be expected to comply with its norms. And they don't. Crime is one of the modes of life of members of the underclass, and many members of this group are young.

Professor Dahrendorf went on to argue that American studies have shown that education is the single most powerful factor in predicting whether an individual has a chance to get out of a condition of severe deprivation, and that entitlement issues have to be dealt with in their own right. He ended his lecture with a challenge:

The question is, who will make the underclass his or her cause? Since I believe in the politics of interest, and see nothing wrong with it, I do not find it easy to answer the question. It will probably have to be by people who have nothing to fear directly, but are concerned about the erosion of citizenship because of its consequences for all.

Professor Dahrendorf's challenge applies to all of us who exercise any form of public ministry, leadership or service. Among us are a number of committed Christians whose public service is an expression of their personal Christian discipleship. For such people the 'yah-boo' of party politics holds no appeal. There is no smirk of satisfaction at the powerlessness of opposition in the face of pre-arranged decisions.

They recognize that decency and good sense come to the fore when men and women are treated with justice and with mercy—when we can all value ourselves without devaluing others.

They don't find their moral standards in a party or a principle, but in a person—in the mind of Christ. That is why I would urge that all such people should find time to read and ponder the words and works of Christ, in the Gospels of Matthew, Mark, Luke and John.

23

COMMUNITY AND RACE RELATIONS

Sermon preached in St Paul's Cathedral, London, 18 July 1976

> 'What share do we have in David? We have no inheritance in the son of Jesse. To your tents, O Israel!'
>
> 1 Kings 12:16

One Sunday I was stopped in the street in Shepherd's Bush by another West Indian. He was carrying a Sunday newspaper which had given front page coverage to the view of a clergyman who wanted all black people repatriated on the grounds that Britain was becoming a nation of liquorice allsorts.

'How is it?' this other West Indian said to me, 'that a church which can defrock a clergyman for fornication, which is only human weakness, can do nothing about a priest who is preaching hate when he should be preaching love?'

Some time before that I had gone to visit a fellow Barbadian who had preceded me to this country. Although he was a regular churchgoer in Barbados, here he never darkened a church door. He wasn't bitter, only very perplexed. 'Since I have come here,' he said, 'and seen how double-dealing these people are, how they smile with you and pat you on the shoulder while they are doing you down, I am afraid to trust the Bible. After all, they gave us the Bible, didn't they? How do I know that they haven't doctored the Bible to suit themselves?'

I remember a serious discussion I had with a middle-aged Englishwoman who was a pillar of the Church. She had been a churchwarden for many years, and she was a Sunday and weekday communicant who practised Christian stewardship and covenanted. She even came to evensong on Sundays! She was no caricature racist. But she argued firmly that black people just had to be inferior, since she could not conceive of a situation in which such large numbers of white people could be subdued by such comparatively small numbers of black people (and kept that way)—in the same way as white people lorded it over black people in Africa and elsewhere. 'The spirit of the white man just wouldn't stand for it,' she said.

Nearly twenty years ago, at the World Council of Churches Assembly in Nairobi, I listened to a heart-rending plea from an African churchman which found an echo in my own situation. 'In Southern Africa we are groaning under the oppression of white racism. It is the one thing that our young people can see before their very eyes. How is it that the Communist countries are the countries willing to help us free ourselves from this oppression, while the Christian countries are the ones helping our oppressors? How can we commend Christianity to our children in the face of this situation?'

Those four situations throw some light on the dilemma facing any thinking black man today who desires, however shakily, to give his allegiance to Christ. He knows that at the heart of most of the world's political problems, and the problems of starvation, disease and misery, is the fact that a minority of the world's people, whom we call 'white', have seized a monopoly of the world's resources. And, whether they are in the majority or minority, in America, Europe or Africa, white people so control and adjust the laws, rules or conventions, that they continue to have more than a fair share of the earth's resources.

Black people know that this is no accident or coincidence; that this is possible only because there exists an understanding which transcends culture, language and distance, and that this understanding commands a greater loyalty than does the revelation of Jesus Christ, whose life and teaching clearly show that all men are brothers and that racism is a sin.

The African will have observed that the white missionary still seems to have more in common with the white, drunken, brawling, promiscuous commercial or service man on the mission station than he has with the native who is a paragon of sobriety and church attendance.

Christianity, we know, is a religion of particularity. We believe that at a specific time in human history God became Man in the person of Jesus Christ. So Christians can understand that even within the context of timelessness and the eternal, there can be decisive moments in history. Therefore we need to take seriously the proposition that the black man is now awake to the mechanics of illusion and deception, and that Christianity must take its place with all the other tools used by white oppression, under the microscope that is half-cynicism and half-hope.

Then there is the task of reconstruction. We have all met the irritating person who, in conversation, insists on finishing our sentences for us, often with words we would never use, and expressing sentiments the very opposite of those we hold. When this happens, more often than not we say 'Quite, quite,' and drift to the far corner of the room. The task facing the black Christian is a mammoth one. He (or she) has to find out if the knotted, jumbled package which has been handed to him under the name of Christianity contains anything that can be salvaged.

What happens if he dispenses with the two-minute silence on Remembrance Sunday? Suppose she expresses doubt about those feet in ancient time walking upon England's mountains green? If perchance that dragon that St George slew was no more substantial than the smoke he was supposed to breathe, or if, with no colonial governor to read the lesson at Morning Prayer, he quietly dropped the passage—'Slaves, obey your masters in the Lord, for it is right?'

Should any or all of these things happen, would anything be left? Pity the black man if you will, as his fingers tug and tug at the strings of this package. Hold your breath or look away, if you want, but please do not rush up to him to take it from his grasp, or tell him how he should set about it—for then, like any other well-bred and dignified man, he may walk away, and leave it in your hands. Please do not finish our sentences for us.

The Gospel has many hard sayings which we black people cannot ignore. It calls on us to share in a ministry of reconciliation. If we know what others do not seem to know, namely that race and colour are a divine gift, that it is part of our personhood for which we are thankful and in which we rejoice, then it is easier for us to see that we races and peoples are meant to be interdependent and to complement one another.

So whatever may have happened in the past, white people and black people belong together. So on our part there has to be forgiveness and an extended hand of fellowship. We may be sure that these are sentiments which the white world will share—and therein lies the danger. As everyone rushes forward for reconciliation, how can we gently communicate that reconciliation cannot be achieved merely by crying, '"Peace, peace", when there is no peace', that we cannot erect a monument of friendship on the soil of injustice and oppression? How can we avoid misleading the white races into breathing a sigh of relief that perhaps after all we have not caught on, and that it can be business as usual? That is one of our problems.

And there is another one. Somehow, we must communicate to our young that it is possible to value yourself without devaluing others. No easy task this. Where do you begin to undo the damage done to a child who is conditioned into a deep sense of inferiority and self-contempt by a situation where everything to be most coveted is white, everything best is white? How does one shift this imbalance and yet prevent it from rushing violently to the other extreme? Here we need help, for if the task with the individual youngster lies mainly with the black elders, the equally urgent task of examining and correcting the social structure lies with the majority of the members of society, whose accents are recognizably authoritative to the ears of those who can act for good or ill.

In my day-to-day work as a parish clergyman, I find that I am now marrying and later baptizing the babies of young black people who were themselves not old enough to begin school fifteen years ago. These last fifteen years, the period of their greatest self-awareness, have been heavy with debate as to whether or not they should be allowed to share in the life of this country. They have seen more and more legislation passed in response to demands that immigration should first be controlled, then restricted.

They have noted that these demands came from the same people who are now demanding that immigration should be stopped altogether and that black people should be repatriated from this country. Comparatively recent history has shown what the ultimate point to be reached on this road is, once it is accepted that the existence of certain people presents a problem which would not exist if the people did not exist.

So young black people in this society, and their elders, have a right to know if they have any allies within this society, or if indeed they stand alone. They have a right to ask Christians to withdraw the certificate of respectability they have so far given to racist campaigns—a certificate that is on display whenever a churchman or woman mouths the contemporary slogan of the racist campaign.

Yesterday the slogan was 'Numbers are of the essence.' Today it is 'We need to know the limit of our commitment.' What will it be tomorrow?

Instead, Church leaders should state clearly, and without any qualification, that Christ's injunction to his followers 'to love your neighbour as yourself' means, for those followers living in Britain today, a call to share willingly the privileges, problems and potential of life in society with *all* their fellow citizens, irrespective of the colour of their skin or the birthplace of their parents.

Secondly, Christians should remember that public opinion is made up, not of what people think, but of that section of their thoughts that they express, and they must speak up, whenever possible, for a just and tolerant multi-racial society. Christians who are part of the silent majority on this issue are part of the sickness rather than part of the cure.

Thirdly, Christians should meet in groups to study the presence and effect of racism in our society, and not merely to congratulate themselves on not being as other men are.

No doubt you are curious to know what 1 Kings 12:16 has to do with all this, so let me give you the context. King Solomon, in order to keep up his standard of living, and as a hedge against inflation, had oppressed his subjects with heavier and heavier taxes. When his son Rehoboam succeeded him, the poor people from the north politely asked that he should get off their backs. But Rehoboam was proud of his ancestry, of the days when his country was great, and he decided to stand firm and make no concessions. It was only then, because they were driven to it, that the oppressed people of the north uttered the words recorded in 1 Kings 12:16:

'What share do we have in David? We have no inheritance in the son of Jesse. To your tents, O Israel!'

24

REMEMBRANCE SUNDAY

Sermon preached at the Civic Service in Fairfields Hall, Sunday 9 November 1986

Each year, on this Remembrance Sunday, we make a point of calling to mind the many thousands of people who died in the two wars known as the First and Second World Wars. Many of those people who died, especially in the Second World War, gave their lives as their way of saying 'No' to the kind of world they did not want.

Almighty God, in his wisdom, created a world of many peoples, nationalities and ethnic groups. He revealed himself fully to mankind, by becoming human as the son of a Jewish woman, and Jesus Christ consistently taught that a man's duty is to love God with all his heart, and to love his neighbour as himself. Furthermore, a man's neighbour is his fellow human being, irrespective of that person's national or ethnic origin.

But in our lifetime a small group of men had other ideas, and they set out to re-order the world. Adolf Hitler and those around him wanted a world in which their own nation would always be the top nation, and their own ethnic group would be a 'master race', ruling all others. To achieve this end they set out in cold blood and in a calculated manner to exterminate people of different ethnic groups and nationalities. The Nazi concentration camps, the gas ovens, the surgical experiments on human beings, marked new depths of man's inhumanity to man.

Thank God, they were defeated in their designs, but not before many millions had lost their lives in the effort to defeat them. British lives were given; Russian lives were given; African, Asian and many other lives were given; Christians, Jews, Sikhs, Muslims, Hindus, Communists and many other faiths were among the dead. Black men and women, white and brown, all laid down their lives to prevent a Fascist and racist domination of the world and to preserve freedom as they knew and loved it.

It is a long time now since the Second World War ended, and some people are beginning to forget. Some years ago, one of the competitors in a contest to find the most glamorous grandmother was aged 33, so she, now a grandmother, was not even born when the war ended. Many of the visible signs of war are disappearing, as new buildings take the places of those destroyed by bombing. The war, and the political events surrounding it, are now taught as history, and children in school write about it in much the same way as they might write about Napoleon or William the Conqueror or Hannibal.

There is therefore the possibility that people may 'know about' the war in much the same way as they 'know about' all these other things, without much consciousness of its significance and relevance to their own daily lives in these times. So it is good that at least once every year we should be asked to remember.

Remembrance. This is a word with which Christians should be very familiar. Sunday after Sunday we hear the priest, taking bread and wine, repeat the words of Christ: 'Do this in remembrance of me.' And when we share in this ritual we know that we are not commemorating some dull, lifeless event from the distant past, but that we are in real communion with the living Lord Jesus, sharing with someone who is present in our midst. Because in biblical usage the word 'remembrance' has a particular meaning. To remember something is to make it once more active in our lives—for good or ill.

All these years later, the kind of world rejected by those who gave their lives in the struggle against Nazism and Fascism is once again being offered to new generations who did not know the horror of concentration camps or the experiments carried out on human beings to produce the Nazi idea of the perfect type.

I have seen, on television, groups of young people in Germany openly declaring that Hitler was right, and that the accounts of the concentration camps were stories invented by the Jews. The leader of the National Front in France was quoted as saying that the death of five million Jews was a mere detail of the war, and it is significant that at least one influential person in this country is anxious to give respectability to this man and to his views.

Here in this country we have Fascist groups who boast about their ideology and presume upon widespread political support. By their statements, policies, slogans and graffiti they encourage verbal and physical attacks upon citizens of this country whose colour or ethnic group they do not approve of.

Today, in Britain, if our remembrance of those who stood shoulder to shoulder and fell alongside each other in wartime in the struggle against Fascism (irrespective of their colour, class or creed) is to mean anything, it must include a determination that such costly sacrifices must not be demanded again.

Wherever racist bigotry rears its head, whether in the polished accents of some politicians, or in the crude shouts of some trouble-makers at football matches, people of goodwill and decency must speak up against it, to ensure that it gains no further ground in our political process or support from our young people.

We best remember the glorious dead when, in our time, we live by and keep alive the ideals for which they died—ideals of freedom, faith, brotherhood, justice and human dignity.

25

CHILDREN

Sermon preached on Sunday 16 May 1993 at a service of thanksgiving to mark the centenary of the National Society for the Prevention of Cruelty to Children (NSPCC) in Croydon Parish Church

The dominant characteristic of Christian worship is thanksgiving. This is not only because we recognize that our relationship with God, who is our creator and the source of all that we are and all that we have, is one of dependence, but also because we recognize him to be a loving Father whose generosity is not elicited by our worthiness but issues from his own love for us.

That love was shown supremely in the gift of our Saviour Jesus Christ, whose life, death and resurrection opened the way for us human beings to share in the life of God.

It is significant that the act of worship which Christ himself instituted centred on thanksgiving. He took bread and wine, gave thanks to the Father, broke the bread, and shared them among his friends. So we call it the Eucharist, which means thanksgiving.

There is no better way of marking a great human achievement than an act of worship. In this way, we demonstrate that whatever part we may have played in such an achievement was played in cooperation with God.

This is not to belittle the human contribution. Perhaps you know the story of the farmer in the outback of Australia who had inherited a veritable wilderness. After years of hard work the wilderness had become a fertile farm. He was being visited one day by the local parson, who looked out over the fields and said to the farmer, 'It is a great miracle you have wrought in this place—you and God together.' 'Yes,' agreed the farmer, 'but you should have seen it when God had it to himself!'

The great human achievement for which we are giving thanks to God in this act of worship this afternoon is the first hundred years of existence and service of the National Society for the Prevention of Cruelty to Children. We give thanks for the vision and foresight of its founders, and for the generosity of its benefactors and the dedication of its workers.

At a time and in an age when in many places human life was short and brutish, when there was widespread resignation to the ravages of poverty and disease, including epidemics, it would have been easy for the well-to-do to think only of looking after their own children, with scant regard to the fate of poor children.

Instead, thanks to the godly inspiration of persons such as Benjamin Waugh, T.F. Agnew, Lord Shaftesbury and others, many such people came to recognize that children are God's gift to the whole human race, and their care and nurture should be the concern and responsibility of the whole community. Incidentally, I hope the Society will consider changing its name (not initials) to 'The National Society for the Protection and Care of Children'.

In many African communities today, and certainly in the Caribbean society in which I grew up, this is considered a self-evident fact. The present Bishop of Lichfield, Keith Sutton, recounts a revealing incident in Uganda when he was teaching there. He was driving his car, and had allowed his small children to sit on the roof of the car. He was stopped by a group of outraged African women. 'These are *our* children,' they remonstrated with him, 'and you have no right to put their lives at risk in this way!' They did not see children as the private property of individual parents but as God's gift to the whole community for its renewing and survival. The impact of this fundamental truth is all the greater when we realize that these African women were black, and Keith Sutton and his children white.

Today in Britain we need to reassert this truth. Our obsession with privatizing everything in sight means that more and more things are seen as private property and fewer and fewer things are seen as gifts from God and, of course, there is that notorious statement, 'there is no such thing as society, only individuals and families'. So children have come to be regarded as the private property of their parents, and more than once I have heard it said that 'People who can't afford children shouldn't have them.'

Thank God he does not see things this way. He knows that poor parents are capable of the greatest sacrifices, will endure the greatest deprivation, and if necessary will subject themselves to great pain and humiliation in their care and concern for the children they love so much. And often it is parents of this sort who are most happy to see their children live lives of service to the whole community rather than concentrate on amassing individual fortunes. It would be interesting to identify the numbers of social workers, missionaries, nuns and voluntary workers overseas who were brought up in large, poor families.

It is significant that an act of worship in church is sometimes called a *service*. To worship anyone is to please him by serving him, and to worship God is to please God by serving him. As Christians, our moral standard is the mind of Christ, and it is to Christ that we turn when we want to know what is right and what it is that pleases God. In the second lesson from St Matthew's Gospel (25:31–46) which the Mayor has just read for us, Christ makes it clear that it is ministry to those who are most vulnerable in our society which best pleases God. And who can doubt that children are among the most vulnerable of God's creatures?

I do applaud our current concern for the environment, for whales and for animal rights. But it did strike me as ironic a few months ago when the plight of a young couple with two children and a dog was featured on television. Their home had been repossessed and they were having to live in sub-standard accommodation provided for homeless families. After the television programme there were over a hundred phone calls offering a home for the dog! No mention of the children.

Where do we go from here? Regrettably, today three out of five children born in the world still die before the age of five. Each day forty thousand people, many of them children, die of starvation and malnutrition-related diseases. Each night half the people in the world, including children, go to bed hungry. All this despite the efforts of UNESCO, Save the Children Fund, the churches and occasional efforts such as Bob Geldof's 'Live Aid'.

Somewhere there are women and men being called by God to do for the world's children today what Benjamin Waugh and others did for the children of this country a hundred years ago. Let us pray that such women and men are not daunted by the size of the task or the difficulties of language, bureaucracy or sheer human sin across international boundaries, but will hear God's call and take the first necessary steps in some new international effort to make the world more hospitable for the greatest treasures of the human race—its children.

26

VALUE

Thought for the Day, BBC Radio 4, broadcast on 2 March 1972

Many West Indians, both in this country and in the West Indies, display on the walls of their homes certain printed maxims, or quotations from the Bible which they have found helpful or inspiring. Two such favourites are: 'God is Love' and 'God is the head of this house.' But I remember from my childhood one which, although it made no mention of God, was still very popular. It read: 'Value thyself, and thou shalt be valued.'

Now at first glance this maxim seems to do no more than state the obvious, because don't we all value ourselves—perhaps in some cases a little too much? But it's when we consider how this is put into practice that we realize its deeper implications. How *do* we value ourselves?

For some people of deep religious conviction it is enough to know that in the eyes of God they, as individuals, are unique and valuable, and that they are loved by God in a way that is special to them. But not all of us are Christians.

For some others, a well-preserved record of their ancestry provides the answer. From childhood they have been conditioned to believe that successive generations of their family have made a peculiar contribution to the world as it is today, and the maintenance of this contribution is now their special responsibility. But not all of us have ancestors who fought in the Battle of Hastings.

I think that for the vast majority of people self-evaluation lies in gauging the reactions of other people with whom they come into contact. The tramp, or the down-and-out, for example, has got a reputation for being shifty-eyed and incapable of looking people in the eye. I believe that he does this, not because he is basically dishonest or necessarily ashamed of what he is, but as a means of protection against the contempt he reads in the eyes of the people with whom he has to deal.

Now, although the case of the tramp is an extreme case, the same is true—in varying degrees—for most of us (except perhaps for those who have the protection of certain identifiable forms of dress or speech).

With this in mind I want to stress the importance of civil servants and others whose 'clients' are recipients of various kinds of social welfare benefits. It may be that the person across the counter, trudging from employment office to housing office, from housing office to dole queue, from dole queue to fish-and-chip shop, is still clinging desperately to some remnant of self-respect. A single 'incident' may remove the final thread, and plunge him to the conclusion that his very existence constitutes a problem and a nuisance for other people. It is out of this conclusion that the worst excesses of anti-social behaviour are born.

Yet it would be wrong to suggest that it is only those who are deprived of material necessities who harbour doubts about their self-value. It is inevitable that the more people are caught up in the pursuit of wealth, the less time they will have to cultivate the friendship of those who cannot contribute in some way or other to this purpose of their life. So it may well be the person of integrity and high ideals who finds himself brushed aside while, in the words of the Psalmist, 'the ungodly flourishes like a green bay-tree'.

It is so important for such a person to realize that his loneliness is not due to some intrinsic shortcoming, and will therefore be a chronic condition. All of us want to feel wanted, and some day perhaps we will. But in the meantime, it is infinitely better to lose our loneliness in the service of those whose self-respect is also at risk, than to dwindle into nothingness and despair because we have not been solicited by the unscrupulous.

However unfashionable it may be, it is better to be a do-gooder than a vegetable. If you value yourself, you will be valued. You are too good to go to waste.

27

NEW CROSS FIRE MEMORIAL SERVICE

Sermon preached in Central Hall, Westminster, on Sunday 17 May 1981 at the memorial service for the thirteen young people who died in the New Cross fire on 18 January 1981

> The king was deeply moved and went up to the roof-chamber over the gate and wept, crying out as he went, 'O, my son! Absalom my son, my son Absalom! If only I had died instead of you! O Absalom, my son, my son.'
>
> 2 Samuel 18:33 (NEB)

King David was a man surrounded by loyal friends and he had many, many children. One of his sons, Absalom, tried to take over his father's kingdom, and was killed by David's loyal friend, Joab. But instead of being grateful to the friend who had saved his life, David was overcome with grief at the death of his son, and so gave voice to the heart-rending lament which I have just read: 'O my son! Absalom my son, my son Absalom! If only *I* had died instead of you. O Absalom, my son, my son.' It didn't matter how many other children David had. The thought of one of his children murdered in this way left him a broken man. He never really recovered.

I am reminded also of another old man—an African in Ian Smith's Rhodesia—and of what he said just before he was shot for harbouring a so-called 'terrorist'. He was not apologetic for having given the guerrilla food. He answered simply: 'He was my son. He came home.'

Every parent lives daily with the knowledge that his or her child may die—from illness or by accident. And when it does happen there is much grief. But when naked human sin snatches a child's life away there is grief of another order. Only those who have themselves had this experience can appreciate that tormenting pain, those dull aches, that emotional hunger which cannot be satisfied, which are the parents' daily lot, awake or asleep. That is the sentence which has been passed on the parents of:

> *Lillian Rosalind Henry, Patricia Johnson, Humphrey Brown, Gerry Paul Francis, Owen Wesley Thompson, Andrew Gooding, Peter Campbell, Glen Powell, Lloyd Hall, Patrick Cummings, Steve Collins, Paul Ruddock, Yvonne Ruddock.*

Our presence here this afternoon is a tiny indication of our wish to help in any way we can—to stand with them, and to say that in a sense these children were our children too, so the whole community has suffered loss. And we thank God for those who escaped from that fire with their lives, even though they and their parents may well bear the physical and emotional scars of this experience for the rest of their lives. Today they and their parents will not begrudge the tributes we pay to their dead companions because, please God, we will find other means of showing them how much we love them and treasure them, and will always do so.

It is at such times as this that we have cause to be grateful for our knowledge of God's presence with us. Those of us who were born thousands of miles away from this country, and who left the security of familiar surroundings to cross the sea in order to carve out a new life here, do not doubt that God has guided us, supported us and protected us from that day until this. And even in this tragedy, we know that he knows, and understands, and cares. He, too, is a parent. He, too, had a son who was killed. And that is why today we can turn to him and ask what would he have us do.

People who do not know God, or who see life in this world as the only life, or the only reality, try in various material ways to raise memorials to those who die. Sometimes they name buildings after them, or plant trees, or erect plaques, or organize anniversary events. But those thirteen young people who died on 18 January have already given *us* more than we can ever give them. They have given us a recognition of our common struggle. What will we do with this recognition?

There are three very powerful emotions which unite people and communities, and sometimes give them a strength which they did not know they possessed. With this strength they can build or they can destroy. The three emotions are love, hate, and grief.

If a community is united in hate, it can only destroy, and God knows there is more than enough hate around already. It must find a scapegoat and use its strength and unity to destroy the innocent scapegoat.

If a community is united in love, it can only build, for love seeks the welfare of all.

If a community is united in grief, it can choose either to build or to destroy. It can be so concerned with itself, so offended at its hurt that it strikes out in blind anger at everyone and everything. On the other hand, it can be strengthened in a determination to make the world a better place for everyone.

When God's son knew that he was about to be killed, he had a message for his friends. He told them: 'This is my commandment—love one another as I have loved you. There is no greater love than this, that a man should lay down his life for his friends.'

Let *that* be the message which our thirteen children have given to us—their mothers, fathers, brothers, sisters, cousins, friends and neighbours: 'Love one another.' If we heed their message, then their memorial will not be in bricks and mortar, or in newspapers, but in our hearts. And in the life of a healthy, vibrant community which knows no fear, because love destroys fear. Then:

They shall not grow old, as we that are left grow old;
Age shall not weary them or the years condemn.
At the going down of the sun, and in the morning,
We will remember them; we will remember them.

28

LAURIE CUNNINGHAM

Sermon preached at the memorial service for Laurie Cunningham, in Southwark Cathedral, 1 October 1989

In many West Indian homes it is common to find printed verses from the Bible, or sayings inspired by such verses, prominently displayed on the walls. One such saying goes like this: 'I shall pass through this world but once, therefore any good that I can do, let me do it now.'

This is really a version of St Paul's words to Christians in Galatia: 'While we have the time, let us do good to all' (Galatians 6:10) and it is part of the lesson which is usually read at harvest festival services, as a reminder that for human lives also there comes a time of harvest when we no longer have time.

> Do not be deceived; God is not mocked, for you reap whatever you sow. If you sow to your own flesh, you will reap corruption from the flesh; but if you sow to the Spirit, you will reap eternal life from the Spirit. So let us not grow weary in doing what is right, for we will reap at harvest-time, if we do not give up. So then, whenever we have an opportunity, let us work for the good of all...
>
> Galatians 6:7–10 (NRSV)

When we walk through a cemetery we sometimes see, in place of the traditional cross at the head of a grave, a pillar which gives the impression that it has been broken off. This is not a Christian symbol but a borrowing from Greek thought, suggesting that the dead person's life has been broken off before it could come to full fruition. But we Christians believe with God it is not the length of life that counts, but the quality of that life. Longevity is not a reward for goodness, neither is an early death a punishment for wrongdoing.

What God prizes is that in the time allotted to us here on earth, we should spare no effort in being and doing what he wants us to be and to do. The Lord Jesus was only thirty-three years old when he was crucified. And many of us will never forget the prophetic words of the late Martin Luther King just before he was shot dead. 'Like anyone else, I would like to live a long life. Longevity has its place. But for me it doesn't really matter now—I only want to do God's will.'

It is God's will for each of us that in the time we have we should do as much good as we can.

Sportspersons are particularly well placed to do good. It is said that one of the inalienable rights with which the Creator has endowed humankind is the *pursuit of happiness*. And sportsmen give a lot of happiness to others. Just by excelling at their chosen sport, combining the mental power of quick thinking with physical strength, speed and skill, they can cause young men to see visions and old men to dream dreams. This was certainly true of Laurie Cunningham.

When I was a curate in Shepherd's Bush over twenty-five years ago I was (as I still am today) an ardent Queen's Park Rangers supporter. But my vicar, who was from the Midlands, was a strong West Bromwich fan. So I used to wonder silently: 'Can any good thing come out of West Bromwich?' Indeed, I was in the crowd at Wembley in 1967 when Alec Stock's third division Queen's Park Rangers defeated first division West Bromwich to win the League Cup!

But then came Laurie Cunningham—brilliant on the wing, with by-line play that we had not seen since Eddie Gray in the glory days of Don Revie's Leeds United! Even I had to admit: 'This boy is a genius—even though he doesn't play for QPR!' He certainly gave a lot of people a lot of happiness. He did us all good.

There is another way in which sportsmen and sportswomen can do good. It is significant that virtually every news bulletin nowadays is followed by a sports report. Only a few minutes after we have been told what Presidents Gorbachev and Bush are doing we are also told what Steffi Graf and Seve Ballesteros and Ian Botham are doing. However much sportspersons might prefer to be private persons, they are projected as persons of public importance, and their actions and opinions can make a lasting impression upon a large number of people, especially young people. They may not choose to be role-models, but role-models they become. Their choice lies in being *good* role-models or *bad* role-models. So what a sports personality says and does about drugs or apartheid is very important.

Laurie was a good role-model for many young black footballers. There was a sense in which he showed that even though there will be obstacles it is still possible for a black footballer to reach the top. That is, not only to play for his country, but at a time when European clubs were head-hunting the best English players, to be chosen by one of the top European clubs. All this required not only intelligence and skill (which he had in abundance) but discipline and hard work. Like others who have followed him since, he had to keep a cool head in the face of racist jeers and taunts from that undesirable element in the crowd that our game of football can well do without.

There is a way in which all of us who are here this evening to thank God for Laurie Cunningham can do good while we have the time. It is by working consciously to make our society a truly multi-ethnic society in which there is equality of opportunity with cultural diversity in an atmosphere of mutual appreciation. Just as football enabled a talented black person to reach the top and represent this country in the international arena, so must politics, the civil service, law, the Church, industry and commerce do the same. And each of us has a part to play in this.

Now, whether we are setting out to travel to the moon or merely heading for the nearest pub, in either case we have to take the first step. The first step is for each of us to ask ourselves the question: 'Would I like a black person to be where I am today?' Then you must decide what is the first step you are going to take to bring this about. If in the years to come you have the satisfaction of seeing this take place, the good that you have done will have been your personal tribute to the memory of Laurie Cunningham—sportsman and role-model.

29

SOUTHWARK DIOCESE HOUSING ASSOCIATION

Speech at the launch of the Southwark Diocese Housing Association at Lambeth Palace, 11 December 1991

Your Grace, Mrs Carey, ladies and gentlemen: There is a story about a bishop who was paying a formal visit to one of his vicars. He was met by the vicar's little son, who looked him over and then asked, 'Where is your trumpet?' Somewhat surprised, the bishop said he did not have a trumpet. 'Oh,' said the disappointed little boy, 'but my dad says you are always blowing your own trumpet!'

Today's launch of Southwark Diocese Housing Association gives me a choice of no fewer than three trumpets—as a churchman, as a board member of the Housing Corporation and as a member of Southwark Diocese.

First as a churchman. A high proportion of the more than two thousand registered housing associations in this country owe their origin to Christians who, although they themselves enjoyed comfortable homes, were impelled to act to provide homes for people whose slender means were not adequate to provide them with homes in keeping with their God-given human dignity.

In the late sixties and early seventies I was myself a founder member of three such associations. In particular I remember the Shepherd's Bush Association, which began with a committee comprising the vicar of the parish in which I was an honorary curate (while serving as the Bishop's Officer in Race Relations), the two churchwardens, some other people we had recruited and myself, with my wife doing the secretarial work and using the parish's typewriter and duplicating machine—all unpaid of course.

I still remember our satisfaction when, with our own hands, we laid the lino in our first property and moved in the first tenants. Today the Association provides more than 2,500 homes! Also, when (as a Board member of the Housing Corporation) I visit the various regions, I am gratified to find that many of the committee members and workers in the various housing associations are active, practising Christians. Thanks be to God.

Secondly, as a board member of the Housing Corporation which is given responsibility for registering, supervising and funding housing associations, I am encouraged by the response of associations to the Board's insistence on highest standards and *value for people* (Bishop Ronnie Bowlby's phrase) secured through value for money. I am encouraged also that today's harsh economic climate has not disheartened those who are concerned with the plight of persons in greatest need but instead has made us more determined to provide homes for elderly people, homeless people, differently-abled people and others such as refugees and minority ethnic communities.

So you will understand why the Housing Corporation welcomes this distinctive initiative, and would encourage the several local authorities in South London to give it every support. It is an initiative worthy of emulation, and could be a model for other dioceses and churches to make land available for affordable housing. The Association will not receive any special favours from the Housing Corporation to the disadvantage of any other Association, but can be assured of a fair hearing and a proper consideration of solid bids for substantial allocations.

Thirdly, as a Bishop in Southwark Diocese, I am proud of the tenacity with which (encouraged by our former Diocesan Bishop, Ronald Bowlby) our Bishop's Council, Diocesan Synod and particular members of the Diocese have caught this vision, kept their eyes on the prize and inched their way towards its attainment. It has been a true essay in cooperation.

It is sometimes said that the proof of the pudding is in the eating. In some cases, however, the proof lies, not so much in the eating as in its long term effects on the digestive system! It is our hope that both are true for the Southwark Diocese Housing Association. That is to say, not only should it provide new homes itself, but it should so inspire similar initiatives that the whole Housing Association movement is galvanized by the release of church land for affordable housing.

So we thank you and Mrs Carey for hosting this launch, your Grace, which elevates a Southwark Diocese effort for the attention—for good, we hope—of the wider Church. Thank you.

Section Four: Good News and Evangelism

30

AGENDA FOR THE CHURCH

Sermon preached when installed as Rural Dean of East Lewisham, at St Laurence, Catford, 28 September 1977

In the course of his ministry on earth our Lord Jesus had many, many disciples. For example, on at least one occasion he sent no fewer than seventy of them out on a mission. But we have come to think of twelve of these disciples, whose names we know—John, James, Peter and the rest—as a group within the general body of disciples. This group of twelve disciples later became apostles and, right from the start, these apostles, because they had been witnesses of the mighty acts of God, namely the life, death and resurrection of Jesus, were accepted by all others as having a peculiar authority, derived from their intimacy with Jesus.

Later, St Paul was to leave us a description of that authority—what it was, where it came from, and how it was to be used. The description is found in 2 Corinthians 4:

> It is not ourselves that we proclaim—it is Christ Jesus as Lord, and ourselves your servants for his sake. For the same God who said—'out of darkness, let light shine', has caused this light to shine within us, to give the light of revelation—the revelation of the glory of God in the face of Jesus Christ.

And St Paul goes on

> But we are no better than pots of earthenware to contain this treasure, and this proves that such transcendent power does not come from us, but is God's alone.

Such then is this apostolic description of those who are ordained within the body of the followers of Christ. Human they are, no more than pots of clay, but commissioned to proclaim Jesus, not merely as a nice person to know, but as *Lord*, someone with authority and power, who has a legitimate claim upon the allegiance of his followers. And in making this proclamation they are actually acting as servants of the people.

It is interesting, too, to see how these first ministers refused to be deflected from this function. The book of Acts, chapter 6, records how certain administrative functions began to take up more and more of the apostles' time, and they were not performing them well anyway. So they said to the believers, 'You find from among yourselves people whom you can trust, who have your confidence. You choose them, but then bring them to us, so that we may give them the necessary authority to get on with these matters of administration. But we ourselves can best serve you by *prayer* and *teaching the Word of God*.

These ordained men were never for one moment in any doubt as to what their role or function should be—no time and motion study was necessary—no Gallup poll. And these priorities, so clearly defined then, remain the priorities for the ordained ministry today. It is by prayer, and by teaching the Word of God, that we proclaim Jesus as Lord, and ourselves as your servants for his sake.

Few who are ordained would suggest that prayer is for ministers alone, or that ministers find it easier to pray than do other members of the church. On the contrary, ministers share with other members of the church the recognition that praying is not easy. Our elder brothers—those first apostles who walked up and down Galilee with Jesus—were in the privileged position of being able to engage him in conversation on any subject which was occupying their mind at the time. They could say to him, 'Lord, we don't want to trouble you, but when you have a minute, could you tell us how we can see Our Father in Heaven?' Or yet again, they could say: 'That was a lovely parable you told the people about the sower and his seed—I liked it. I liked it—but what exactly did it *mean*?' And there and then they could receive their answers on the spot. Not so with us.

And yet the intimacy between our Lord Jesus and the ordained ministers of his Church today must be no less than was the intimacy between him and his first apostles. Such intimacy is born of prayer.

That is why the celebration of the Eucharist must always have first call on the priest's time. In praying the Eucharist we know that Jesus is always present. We know that the Eucharist can never be other than the perfect prayer. For whenever we are tempted to let our lives be dominated by temporary obsessions—our state of health, our loneliness, the welfare of our family and friends, our feelings of hostility against detractors or critics, we can know that the shortcomings and inadequacies of our prayers are filled in with the perfection of his sacrifice. Where the first apostles walked by sight, we later generations must walk by faith, so our prayer reflects our confident conviction that God, who created the world and all that is in it, expressed himself fully and completely, in human terms, in the life, death and resurrection of Jesus Christ; that by laying hold on this belief we become fashioned in the image of this God, whose relationship with us, as with all humankind, is that of Father. That is why we must pray.

And when we turn to the second priority of the ordained minister, namely the teaching of the Word of God, there are some things about which we need to remind ourselves. First, that in teaching the Word of God we *do* the word, rather than *speak* the word. If it is one thing we have learnt from the coming of television and the multiplication of radio stations, it is how meaningless mere words can be. Even worse, words can be manipulated, not merely to conceal the truth, but to project a distortion of the truth.

You may remember the occasion when during the Watergate troubles in America, President Nixon's Press Secretary told newsmen: 'All that I said to you yesterday is now inoperative.' 'Do you mean,' asked one astonished reporter, 'that what you told us yesterday was all lies?' 'I mean,' replied the Secretary, 'that it is now inoperative.' And from that statement he would not budge.

We can no longer assume that when we have gazed earnestly into the television camera and made a statement or when we have preached a sermon on love, we have proclaimed Jesus. We know, and everyone knows, that it costs us nothing to do this, whereas proclaiming Jesus is a demanding activity.

The Word we are teaching is a person who died that others might live; who claimed that those who *lived* the will of God were for him his mother and his brethren. We are teaching a person who was loved and hated in turn by the respectable and by the rabble rousers, and who found that because he loved all people he was often forced to be lonely. So, although we clergymen are no doubt precious in the eyes of God, we should never be precious in our own. And if teaching the Word of God means standing up to the government of the day, or to the National Front, and being hated for it, do we have a choice?

The Church of God in East Lewisham, as in every other part of the world, is God's creation. If God is the kind of God who is concerned only with himself, with his pleasures and his comforts, his independence, his self-security, and if God is worried that to meet humankind's needs would be to make a sacrifice he is not prepared to make, then we are being faithful to such a God when we also do these things.

But if God expressed himself by giving of himself to forgive the sins of sinners, to heal the sick in mind and body, to clothe the naked, feed the hungry, and to stand with the despised and the oppressed, then the agenda for the Church in East Lewisham has already been written. We must continue with this agenda.

31

PREACHING THE GOSPEL

Sermon preached at the annual Croydon Area Episcopal Service in Croydon Parish Church, 21 September 1986.

Stop almost anyone in the street and ask: 'What is the purpose of the Church?' and he or she will answer without any hesitation—'To preach the gospel!' If you ask what that gospel is, a fair number of people will be able to tell you that it is about Jesus Christ and the love of God. It isn't until you ask *how* that gospel is to be preached, and to whom, that you are likely to encounter some disagreement. Because if the person is a Church person he is likely to be affronted by any suggestion that it should be preached to *him*, since he reckons that he knows it already; and if you suggest that *he* should be proclaiming it, he is likely to say that he is not a minister, unless of course he happens to be a minister, in which case he will tell you that preaching the gospel is the mission of the *whole* church!

So perhaps it is better to say to your person: 'Look, I know that the mission of the Church is to proclaim the good news of God's love, and the Church is ministers and lay people together, so *how* are you doing it? Do the ministers proclaim it to the lay people and the lay people proclaim it to the ministers, and does everyone know, when you huddle together, that this is what you are doing?' Huddles are necessary, but no tries are scored in scrums! It is necessary to leave the scrum and travel with the ball!

This is a question of some relevance because for some years now many of our parishes have been engaging in courses and exercises and counselling sessions designed to deepen the faith of Christians, and there is, thank God, a greater awareness of our need to care for one another. At the same time there is a niggling worry that our increasingly secular and materialistic society is not *hearing* the Word of God. We need to ask why.

First of all it seems to me that we, the Church, must refute the notion that wealth and prosperity are necessarily a sign of God's favour and approval. I do not think that in this country there is the crude assertion, so popular in some other places, that wealth and possessions are the rewards with which God blesses those whose prayers he chooses to answer. But neither can it be said that a distinguishing mark of Christians in our society today is our witness, vocal or otherwise, against the almost limitless greed which is now being constantly held up as the desirable driving force for our way of life.

For the past few days we have been reading the prophecy of Amos[1] as the first lesson at Morning Prayer. Amos declares that famine of the Word of God in a land is not *accidental*, but a consequence of certain actions and behaviour. In chapter 8, reading from verse 4, he says:

> Listen to this, you who trample on the needy and try to suppress the poor people of the country, you who say, 'When will New Moon be over so that we can sell our corn, and sabbath, so that we can market our wheat? Then by lowering the bushel, raising the shekel, by swindling and tampering with the scales, we can buy up the poor for money, and the needy for a pair of sandals, and get a price even for the sweepings of the wheat.' Yahweh swears it by the pride of Jacob, 'Never will I forget a single thing you have done... See what days are coming—it is the Lord Yahweh who speaks—days when I will bring famine on the country, a famine not of bread, a drought not of water, but of hearing the word of Yahweh.'
>
> Amos 8:4–7, 11 (JB)

Is this why our society is not hearing the word of God? For the Church in this country the mission field today is the 'mass society', a society characterized by mass production and mass consumption of goods; mass communication in entertainment, news, advertising; and mass crime. It is to this kind of society that the Church must preach love. This is no easy task, because in a mass society, and in public affairs, love must take the form of justice. So every form of justice—economic justice, legal justice, social justice, racial justice, must be the practical concern of Christians and the Church.

Where do we begin? With an examination of our own lives in the light of the teaching of Jesus about material things, and I suggest that there are three basic principles in Our Lord's teaching to guide us.

The first is that *all things belong to God*. This is reported again and again in Holy Scripture. Psalm 24, for example:

> The earth is the Lord's and the fulness thereof, the world and those who dwell therein.

And again:

> For every beast of the forest is mine, the cattle on a thousand hills...
>
> Psalm 50:10 (RSV)

[1] Anglican ministers normally read the Daily Office in the morning and the evening and the Lectionary sets out the readings for each day.

In the parables of Jesus, it is the master who gives the talents, the owner who gives the vineyard to the husbandmen, and so on. It is so important that we see ourselves as stewards of earthly possessions, so that we use them as *God* would want them used. The ultimate ownership of all things is God's, and our own stewardship is for a comparatively short time. Once, when a very wealthy man had died, someone asked: 'How much did he leave?' and was given the correct answer: 'All of it.'

The second basic principle is that *people matter more than things*. If the only way we can make money is by treating people as things, then such riches are wrong in the sight of God. The dignity and worth of human personality cannot be bought and sold. That is why slavery was wrong; why child labour was wrong; why unfettered market forces which disregard human need must always be wrong.

No one should die of hunger simply because he has no money to buy food; or of any illness because he cannot buy the medicines or medical care that would save his life. It is worth recalling the words of Coleridge in 1842 when he was told that cheap labour was necessary to keep costs down and profits up. He said: 'You talk about making this article cheaper by reducing its price from 8 pence to 6 pence. But suppose in doing so you have rendered your country weaker against a foreign foe; suppose you have demoralized thousands of your fellow countrymen and sown discontent between one class of society and another, that article would have been very expensive!' People must always be more important than things.

The third basic principle is that *wealth is always a secondary good at most.* Scripture says that 'the love of money is the root of all evil', and wealth can become an alternative means of salvation. That is to say, we can come to believe that it is possible to buy anything or anyone, and buy ourselves out of any situation. There is even that terrible saying: 'Every man has his price.' It is possible to treat wealth as a measuring rod for everything. You may have heard in the news yesterday that the government is now recommending a tariff of compensation for people who are attacked by thugs: £75 for a bruise; £100 for a black eye; so much for a broken arm, so much for a broken leg, and so on.

The Bible does not say that money itself is the root of all evil: only the love of it. Money can be used for such honourable purposes as the welfare of family and fellow men. But when money is acquired simply to increase status, profits, luxury and pleasure, then it is no longer secondary: it has taken the primary place in life which belongs to God alone. So Christians with incomes and material possessions should see them—in that excellent phrase coined by Canon Gordon Mayo when he was Director of Christian Stewardship in this diocese—as 'God-given resources to be managed for mission'. They are not to be squandered—but neither are they to be hoarded selfishly.

This self-examination should be the starting point of a programme for every parish in our area with this aim: *To integrate the service of faith and the promotion of justice in the one mission.* Believing, praying and doing, receiving and giving must all be aspects of the one mission. And here I must tell you a story. It is about the man who was drowning but was sure God would save him because he had faith. A water-skier saw him struggling and offered to help. 'No,' said the man, 'God will save me.' A man in a rowing boat tried to pull him out: 'No,' he insisted, 'God will save me.' Then a third man, this time in a speed boat, came dashing up, but still he refused. Finally he drowned. As he went under, he said 'Where were you when I needed you, God?' And God replied: 'I sent you water skis, a rowing boat and a speed boat. What did you want? The *Q.E. II*?'

It may be that in the parishes there will be those who say, 'We don't have the resources and we don't know anything about economic justice, or social justice, or racial justice.' But our diocese does employ a lay training team, a Christian stewardship team, a race relations team, a justice and development worker, and a worker with the single homeless—and all these people are your servants. You have only to call upon them. We may not have the *Q.E. II*, but neither do we need it!

Finally, let me encourage you by suggesting that other Christians find it no easier than we do to meet certain demands of the gospel in our society. One of our Southwark priests reported on a Pentecostal service he attended. The leader prayed: 'Lord, we give you our praise' and the people responded 'Amen.' 'Lord, we bring you our sins!' 'Amen,' they all agreed. 'Lord, we give you our lives.' 'Amen,' they shouted. 'Lord, we give you our money.' Dead silence.

32

CHRISTIANITY, OUR GLOBAL FAITH

Sermon preached at St James', New Malden, 28 February 1993

I have been asked to speak to you this morning on 'Christianity, our global faith', and I would begin by reminding you and myself that you and I are religious people. In common with other religious people, such as Muslims, Sikhs, followers of Judaism and others, we believe in the One God who created the universe and all humankind. But in addition, we are 'Christians', because we believe that Jesus, the Son of Mary born in Bethlehem almost two thousand years ago, is the Christ.

We believe Christ to be the interpretation of all human life and history, as the Prologue of St John's Gospel puts it, and to believe in Jesus as Christ is much more than believing facts about Jesus. To believe in Jesus is to believe:

- ***That human life has meaning and purpose. We are not in this world by accident, because we have a place in the eternal plan.***
- ***That the world is built on moral foundations, so there is right and there is wrong. We can know which is which because our moral standard is the mind of Christ.***
- ***That each of us is important, but no more so, and no less so, than the other people God has made. So we should not think too highly of ourselves and too little of other people.***

Finally, we believe that we should order our lives on these beliefs—and let others know why we do so. We shall tell them the good news about the nature and the love of God so that they also will come to accept Jesus as Lord, and greater and greater will be that alignment of human activity with God's will and purpose which we call the kingdom of heaven on earth. This, we believe, is God's will for his world. In that sense Christianity, our faith, is a global faith.

It is important that in commending Christianity to the world we begin not with a creed to be believed called Christianity, or an organization to be defended called the Church, but with Jesus. We preach Christ crucified, whose life and teaching were at one in revealing God to be a God of love, a love that is so inclusive that every one of us has a unique and infinite worth. This love makes nonsense of the world's preference for a system of values which marks some persons out as being more worthy than others, using criteria of birth or achievement or nationality or ethnic group or gender.

From New Testament times it became clear that the good news of Christ had such power and such a transforming effect that people began to covet it for its material rewards. In Acts 8 Simon the Sorcerer offered the apostles money in return for the power to heal people in the name of Jesus.

Consider your own call, brothers and sisters: not many of you were wise by human standards, not many were powerful, not many were of noble birth. But God chose what is foolish in the world to shame the wise; God chose what is weak in the world to shame the strong; God chose what is low and despised in the world, things that are not, to reduce to nothing things that are, so that no one might boast in the presence of God. He is the source of your life in Christ Jesus, who became for us wisdom from God, and righteousness and sanctification and redemption, in order that, as it is written, 'Let the one who boasts, boast in the Lord.'

When I came to you, brothers and sisters, I did not come proclaiming the mystery of God to you in lofty words or wisdom. For I decided to know nothing among you except Jesus Christ, and him crucified. And I came to you in weakness and in fear and in much trembling. My speech and my proclamation were not with plausible words of wisdom, but with a demonstration of the Spirit and of power, so that your faith might rest not on human wisdom but on the power of God.

1 Corinthians 1:26—2:5 (NRSV)

That particular effort was unsuccessful, but the existence of hundreds of Christian churches, groups and sects around the world today is a result of groups of Christians devising their own user-friendly versions of Christianity and putting loyalty to nation or tribe or churchmanship or tradition before loyalty to Christ crucified.

In this country we are in danger of seeing our religion not so much as the local expression of a universal faith called Christianity but more as the religious expression of our national and cultural identity. Because of this we find it difficult to grasp that even in the Anglican Communion the vast majority of Christians, including those coming to the Christian faith as adults in their thousands today, are from African and Asian ethnic groups rather than European.

One of the reasons for this slow understanding is a half-conscious assumption that God rewards Christian virtue and goodness with material blessings. True, we are not as crude as the American 'televangelists' who push this distorted doctrine to its limits and claim to guarantee prosperity, good health and other blessings from God to those who send them money. But as radio and television bring us graphic accounts of the devastation of other countries by floods, drought, famine, war, disease and murderous governments, there are still those who see in this an element of God's judgment upon these nations, and our freedom from such scourges as a reward for our own prudence.

I was made very conscious of this in February 1991, when I was attending the Seventh Assembly of the World Council of Churches in Canberra at the time of the Gulf War. The World Council of Churches is a fellowship of churches which confess the Lord Jesus Christ as God and Saviour according to the Scriptures, and therefore seek to fulfil together their common calling to the glory of the One God, Father, Son and Holy Spirit. There are some 314 churches in this fellowship, and every seven years there is an Assembly of delegates to review, discuss and recommend programmes for making Christ known and for strengthening cooperation between churches with the goal of visible unity.

As the numbers of Christians and churches increase in Africa and Asia, so the World Council of Churches, which at the outset in 1948 was predominantly white, has come to reflect more and more these changes in representation and participation. At the same time these new churches are mainly countries in the southern hemisphere who suffer from a world economic system over which they have no control. The minority white churches are from the rich part of the world, and the others from the poor parts of the world. So there are tensions, and in disagreements over issues there are mutterings that 'He who pays the piper should call the tune.'

It is worth bearing this in mind when we are listening to criticisms of the WCC. At the Assembly itself it was the Gulf War that threw this into sharpest focus. There was not a single person at the Assembly who supported Saddam Hussein or agreed with his invasion of Kuwait. But the vast majority of Christians at the Assembly were conscious that the many young conscripts had had no say in the choice of Saddam as their ruler, and were like tethered goats in the desert who would be blown into a million bits by bombs dropped from planes so high in the sky that they could not see them. And all at the touch of a button by pilots sitting in air-conditioned comfort.

Even the American churches opposed the war. Only the British (led by the Church of England) and Australian delegations attempted to justify it. There was a strong feeling among the other delegates that they did so because their loyalty to the governments of their countries who were involved in the war was greater than their loyalty to Christ.

Christianity is not a global faith merely because in every corner of the globe Christian churches are to be found. It is a global faith because wherever there are people the Spirit of Jesus can be present. It is the Spirit of the One who 'though being in the form of God, did not snatch at equality with God'. The one who said to those around him, 'Greater love has no man than this—that a man should lay down his life for his friends ... You are my friends ... Love one another as I have loved you.' He who prayed while he was being put to death, 'Father, forgive them—they do not know what they are doing.'

Christianity is present in Northern Ireland, not because there are many church services there, but because it shines in a man like Gordon Wilson who prays for his daughter's murderers. It is present in the black mother in South Africa whose nineteen-year-old son was arrested, tortured and killed, who said, 'I ask God to give the years my son would have lived to those who killed him, in order that they may repent and be forgiven.'

Because Christ reaches out to everyone on each side of every barrier, our faith is truly global, and there will be those, even if they stand alone like Christ in the wilderness, who will be true to their crucified Lord. God grant that we be found among their number.

33

TEACHERS AND VOCATION

Sermon preached to teachers in Church schools at the Church of the Good Shepherd, Lee, 11 May 1978

> 'If it is my will that he remain until I come, what is that to you? Follow me!'
>
> John 21:22 (RSV)

You may have heard the story of the American tourist who was passing through a small village after visiting the tomb of Sir Winston Churchill and the birthplace of William Shakespeare. He called out to a passing villager: 'Hey, any important men born in this village?' 'No,' said the villager, 'only babes!'

Unfortunately this preoccupation with status is not confined to American tourists. Many conventions and assumptions in the way our life is organized today accord to some people in the public eye a disproportionate amount of time and importance at the expense of many others who are following even more worthwhile vocations. The power of radio and television adds to this tendency, with the result that all too often human life becomes one endless rat race, as more and more people compete for fewer and fewer places in the spotlight.

It is no longer enough to be *competent* in your work. In terms of personal ambition it is far more helpful to be *well-known*! In such a state of affairs it is not surprising that people who in theory should be working as a team are often in *practice* competing with one another; and that where genuine achievement should evoke pleasure and admiration, and win congratulations from colleagues, instead it provokes only misery, envy and jealousy.

All of this is in sharp conflict with what should be a Christian attitude to *vocation* if we learn the lesson of the incident from which our text is taken. It took place after Our Lord's resurrection, and probably near the end of the forty days when he had appeared and spoken to his disciples (who were soon to become *apostles*) on a number of occasions. By this time they would have grasped the fact that victory was a certainty, that the Kingdom of Christ would take shape for all to see. But they were also aware that there was still work to be done, and awards to attain, and since Christ had produced no 'seating plan' for the heavenly banquet they were curious about their individual destinies.

So when Our Lord told Peter that *his* job was to be a pastor to the end, his immediate concern was to know what job would be going to another of the disciples. His question: 'Lord, what will *this* man do?' produced Our Lord's devastating and uncompromising description of *Christian* vocation: 'If it should be my will that he wait until I come, what is that to you? You follow me.' We can imagine Peter having to swallow very hard.

Always the paramount consideration in Christian vocation is the *will of God*. At any particular time or in any particular place the task to which we are called by God is not necessarily the one we would choose for ourselves, or the one we ourselves believe to be best, or the one we enjoy most. It may even be a task which others, less able than ourselves, have spurned. It may be a task which appears to lose us among many others doing the same thing, described in the same way, always in the shadows, when we yearn more than anything else, if only just for once, to occupy the centre of the stage, and to hear our name on other people's lips.

But our *faith* is that God knows us, loves us and wills the best for us, so it is in doing *his* will that we find the fulfilment that is rightfully ours to have. In accepting our vocation, therefore, our first question is not whether it makes us happy, or whether it makes us useful, or whether it makes us well-known, but whether it is the *will of God for us*. This means that it must be the subject of much prayer and meditation; the constant recourse to the

Scriptures and the Sacraments of the Church, and sometimes to the spiritual guidance of a father-in-God with whom we have been completely honest. There will be times when human considerations, *valid for everyone else except ourselves* will make us want to ask: 'What about her?'—'And what about him?'—'And what about them?' And Christ's answer will be 'What is that to you? You follow me.'

A second consideration about Christian vocation is that it must be compatible with Christian discipleship. What makes Christianity more than a system of thought, or a philosophy, is that it is a religion of a person. This person is God, and also human, so, inspired by *his* Spirit we also follow the example of his life. We cannot therefore imagine that he would call us to a life which he himself would not lead.

I remember some years ago watching a television programme about the wealthy people who lived on an exclusive Channel Island, and listening to an interview with one of them. His estate was surrounded by high walls, and he thought that what was wrong with the world today was that people coveted other people's belongings far too much! He quoted the Ten Commandments to show that God was against the covetous. For his own part, he said that he had worked hard for everything that he had. It did not seem to matter to him that he had made his money as an arms salesman. In other words, by generating and encouraging the need for guns, bombs and other methods of human destruction, and then by meeting that need, he had become wealthy.

I could not see Our Lord following that way of life, or calling on others to do so. So Christian vocation must be compatible with Christian discipleship.

So from two clearly defined angles the Christian teacher is following a vocation. First, it is clear that Our Lord Jesus, in his own life and ministry, gave teaching the highest priority. What is more, he could not have been unaware of the value of the written word as a means of communication, yet he wrote no scroll, or letter, biography or book of any kind. Why? Could it be that he believed that in teaching one gives of oneself, and that what is taught is authenticated by the daily, living witness of the teacher?

Certainly today's RE teacher must find this question inescapable. Unlike some others, he or she cannot dismiss those fits of depression which grip us all from time to time with a cynical shrug of the shoulder: 'Oh well, it is only what I do for a living—I don't have to believe any of it!'

Secondly, for the individual Christian, vocation lies, not merely in the job we do, but in the way we do it. Christian vocation lies in being motivated by the desire to please God in all we do, so our work becomes an expression or vehicle of that motivation. The Christian teacher with a sense of vocation is not necessarily more gifted than other teachers, or more successful than others, but none can be more conscientious, and none is better rewarded, than he or she is. So when, occasionally, tempted to gaze enviously at those in the public eye, or tempted to forget that the rat race is essentially designed for rats (and so the rats do better at it) he or she must hear Our Lord speaking as he did to Peter, saying, 'What is that to you? You follow me!'

May I leave you with some words I came across many years ago, in a book by my Barbadian schoolmaster Gordon Bell? They go like this.

The artist works on canvas, the sculptor in marble; the potter in clay—all of which must some day fall to pieces. So, too, must be the fate of the worker in wood, and the worker in metal. But the teacher—his material is the living being fashioned in the image of His Maker. To help fill a mind with knowledge, and a heart with understanding—that is to share creation with God.

May God bless you in your work for him.

When they had finished breakfast, Jesus said to Simon Peter, 'Simon, son of John, do you love me more than these?' He said to him, 'Yes, Lord; you know that I love you.' He said to him, 'Feed my lambs.' A second time he said to him, 'Simon, son of John, do you love me?' He said to him, 'Yes, Lord; you know that I love you.' He said to him, 'Tend my sheep.' He said to him the third time, 'Simon, son of John, do you love me?' Peter was grieved because he said to him the third time, 'Do you love me?' And he said to him, 'Lord, you know everything; you know that I love you.' Jesus said to him, 'Feed my sheep. Truly, truly, I say to you, when you were young, you girded yourself and walked where you would; but when you are old, you will stretch out your hands, and another will gird you and carry you where you do not wish to go.' (This he said to show by what death he was to glorify God.) And after this he said to him, 'Follow me.'

Peter turned and saw following them the disciple whom Jesus loved, who had lain close to his breast at the supper and had said, 'Lord, who is it that is going to betray you?' When Peter saw him, he said to Jesus, 'Lord, what about this man?' Jesus said to him, 'If it is my will that he remain until I come, what is that to you? Follow me!'

John 21:15–22 (RSV)

34

PRAYING FOR OTHERS

From the Southwark Diocesan Calendar for Prayer, 1987

Have you ever been tempted not to pray for some particular person? That is to say, you kneel down and take out your intercession list, and you begin to pray for Desmond Tutu, Allan Boesak and others with them in South Africa.

Then there flashes before your mind's eye the TV picture of this fully armed white policeman barring the way of the weeping black woman who is trying to reach her twelve-year-old son who has just been shot by the police. His words to this mother: 'Let the bastard die!'

You wonder how you can pray for this man's good, but it is not long before another picture takes its place. It is of Christ on the cross.

Father, forgive them, they don't know what they are doing.

Therein lies one of the great benefits of intercessory prayer. It transforms the person who prays. What person can constantly strive to see persons and situations through the eyes of Christ, repeatedly retracing his steps to ensure that his thoughts are thoughts of Christ, and yet remain impervious to the transforming power of such sacrificial love?

Each of us is linked in various ways with various people near and far. This intercession calendar helps us to remember before God people in this diocese and in the worldwide Anglican Communion with whom we are linked in a common struggle to make Christ known.

We look at them through the eyes of Christ and we see how faltering their witness—like ours—is. We see that they need all the help they can get and so we pray for them, as one means of helping in a way we can. To assure them of our prayers is something more than just a nice way to end a letter.

35

FORGIVENESS

Sermon preached at St Peter's, Croydon, Sunday 13 February 1994

> Peter said to Jesus: 'Lord, how often must I forgive my brother if he wrongs me? As often as seven times?' Jesus answered: 'Not seven times, I tell you, but seventy times seven.'
>
> Matthew 18:21

Anyone who believes in the God revealed in Jesus Christ believes in *sin*. To believe in such a God is to believe in a loving Creator who knows what is best for humankind, and whose will is the standards by which human actions are to be measured. The word 'sin' is the translation of the Greek word *hamartia*, which means falling short of the target—as when one shoots an arrow and it falls short. Sin is the falling short, in human behaviour, of God's standards. All human beings, including ourselves, are therefore sinners.

Sins and crimes are not one and the same, although many crimes are also sins. A crime is the breaking of the law which has been made by those who have the authority to make laws on behalf of the nation, and in order to discourage lawbreaking, the lawmakers also prescribe punishments for those who break the laws. For that reason many nation-states are so ordered that crime and punishment go together.

But even where crime is not involved, people with power or authority find punishment useful as a means of controlling the behaviour of weaker persons. For example, many parents have various ways of punishing children when the children break the rules that the parents have made.

It follows that we would all understand that God, who has created the world and humankind, has a perfect right to make rules for us, and to punish us when we break his rules.

In the time of Jesus, the prevailing view among religious teachers was not only that God had this right, but that he did exercise it. In their view disasters which befell people were God's way of punishing those people who had broken his laws either openly or in secret. Religious teachers were so wedded to this theory that even when people were born with some handicap, such as blindness, they argued that such people were being punished for their *parents'* lawbreaking.

Jesus did not dispute that God had such rights. But he showed us that God's attitude to us, his children, was not shaped by *our* behaviour, but by his own nature. It is God's nature to *love*, and his way of winning our compliance with his will is to offer even greater help (or grace) when we fall short of his standards for us. God is the smiling, encouraging mother rather than the scowling, punishing parent! The grace he interposes between our sin and any punishment we deserve is called *forgiveness*.

Our gospel reading this morning draws our attention to this feature of God's relationship with us. It is the story of the woman taken in adultery and brought before Jesus. According to the law she was punishable by death from stoning by her peers, and Jesus was asked if this sentence should be carried out. Although today we may well ask why it was that although it takes *two* to commit adultery, only one—the woman—was being accused, and why it was that her accusers were all men, these questions need not detain us now. Jesus did not attempt to deny the woman's offence or to make excuses for it. He did not even denounce the unfairness of it all. Instead, he showed that both the person who was accused, and those who were accusing her, had all fallen short of the required standards, because no guiltless person could be found to carry out the sentence. His final words to the woman show the proper response to God's forgiveness: 'Go and sin no more.' God's way of weaning us away from our sins is by loving forgiveness.

The teachings of Jesus are replete with encouragement to us to forgive others. He told, with disapproval, the story of the cruel servant who owed a huge debt and could have been sold out by his creditor. The creditor spared him on compassionate grounds, but the same servant found a fellow-servant who owed him a few pence which he was unable to repay, and had him imprisoned for this small debt. Jesus also taught his followers, that in approaching God for his forgiveness, we may recall that for our part we forgive those who trespass against us.

The willingness to forgive is a normal feature of normal Christian living.

The supreme example of forgiveness, as with so many other human experiences, is to be found in the life of Our Lord Jesus Christ. Aged only 33, he could have gone on for many years doing the things he loved doing—healing, teaching, helping people to change their thinking about themselves. He had done no wrong, yet he found himself being put to death on a cross—the work of men who thought this was the best course of action in their own short-term interests. And as if his own physical suffering was not enough, no doubt he could envisage the pain and suffering of generations yet unborn that would result from the actions of these men—the persecution, wars, misguided crusades, terrorism, the bloody hostilities between adherents of different religions, and even within Christendom itself, the factional fighting between Catholics, Orthodox and Protestants.

What punishment could be considered appropriate for those whose selfish actions would lead to such devastation? Since the more spiritually mature a person is, the more that person feels the weight of moral evil, Jesus more than anyone else would know the enormity of the sin they were committing. He saw it all, and seeing it, he prayed: 'Father, forgive them.' That forgiveness was very, very costly.

However tempting it may be for us to label others and ourselves 'guilty' or 'innocent', 'villain' or 'victim', we human beings share a common humanity and are all children of the same sinful Adam. It is as such that with our hands stained with the blood of Jesus, we are beneficiaries of his prayer: 'Father, forgive.'

It is as such that we are guilty of the sins of those who murder children (as is happening in Sarajevo almost every day), murder policemen (as happened in New Addington last week), and all such acts that are as public as the woman taken in adultery. And we are guilty also with those who abuse children, mistreat wives, profit financially from drug addiction, from starvation wages in poor overseas countries; the manufacture and sales of arms—such sins are as secret as the sins of the respectable men who accused the woman before Jesus.

Until we recognize our own complicity and our own selfishness, we will never know the healing power of forgiveness expressed in the words of Jesus: 'Go and sin no more.' When the sinfulness within ourselves takes visible form in other people's despicable and degrading acts, and we are tempted to wreak vengeance and even violence on such unfortunates, may we have the grace to turn our eyes to Jesus on the cross and pray sincerely: 'Lord, we forgive; Help Thou our unforgiving.'

One final thought. In a world of feuds, vendettas and wars of attrition, a future without hope is too frightening to contemplate. It is only out of *forgiveness* that hope can be born.

36

EVANGELISM

Talk given at Rural Deans' and Lay Chairpersons' Consultation held at Wychcroft, a Southwark Diocese training centre, 11–13 January 1991

Evangelism is the telling of good news, and we Christians have appropriated the term 'good news', or 'gospel', to refer to God's action in Jesus Christ.

The simple facts are that a son was born to a humble village girl named Mary, living at that time in occupied Palestine. He was given the very ordinary Jewish name of Jesus, and he worked in a carpenter's shop until he was thirty, and for three years after that he was a wandering preacher. So far as we know he never wrote a book; he never held an office; he never owned a home; he never married or had a family. His preaching attracted large crowds and excited people.

Then public opinion turned against him and his friends ran away. His enemies put him through a mockery of a trial, condemned him and executed him as a common criminal, crucified between two thieves. He died and was buried. After his death and burial his dead body was nowhere to be found. But from time to time he would join his friends in various places, talking and eating with them. When his friends told people about this, and argued that he was the leader God had promised to send to the Jewish people, they were accused of blasphemy, imprisoned, beaten and sometimes killed for making such a claim.

But they persisted, preferring to flee for their lives rather than deny what they themselves had experienced, that is, the presence of Jesus alive after his death. Wherever they went, even while hiding from the authorities, they met to thank God for giving them the privilege of knowing Jesus. They recalled his teaching and tried to put into practice what he said and did. Because they wanted others to share their good fortune, they told anyone who would listen about him—his life and teaching, his death and resurrection, and how they now believed that God had sent him, not only to the Jewish people, but to humankind everywhere. The good news was that because of his sacrificial death, those who believed in him and turned from their present way of life to his were forgiven for all their wrongdoing and made righteous in God's sight. They believed that although unseen, the living Jesus was present with them and within them in Spirit, and that they could call on him wherever they happened to be.

The result of all this was that many other people, of all ages and nationalities, joined in their fellowship. And even though in due course those first witnesses died out, their successors increased in number, travelling all over the then known world. That is how, nearly two thousand years later, in a country where the inhabitants were still living in tribal societies when all this began, a group of us are assembled here to think how best we may tell this good news to those around us in a special effort over the next ten years and for the foreseeable future.

Those are the simple facts. This is not to say that over the centuries learned theologians, historians, philosophers and scientists have not studied, theorized, elaborated and adorned the gospel story. Composers and musicians expressed it so that their hearers have been deeply moved by it. Painters and artists have been inspired so to depict it on canvas that viewers have been transported in wonder and delight. Playwrights and film-makers have taken up the theme and captured their audience's emotions. And architects have designed cathedrals that have made even atheist sceptics speak in hushed tones within their walls.

This reason for all is that in the person of Jesus it is God who became human—and the deepest explorations and probings of scholars and artists and thinkers are struggling to manifest the presence of this same Jesus.

But however flattering to our egos, and however seductive it may be that our sophistication enables us to receive communication from kindred spirits in our own cultures, such probing is not the gospel itself and is no substitute for it. We have all heard sermons in which the learned preacher name-drops incessantly in his references to the works of scholars and theologians, and seems to imply that unless you are familiar with their works the true gospel is beyond your reach. There is even the whiff of a suggestion that these writers (and perhaps the preacher himself) are rather more clever than Jesus was!

The trouble is that we can be vulnerable to this kind of error because we are so conditioned to a stratified society that we may not question the idea of God treating some of his children more favourably than others. It is as though we are saying, 'Of course, we are all equal in God's love—but some are more equal than others!'

Yet if the gospel is for *all* humankind of all levels of capability—and who can doubt that it is—then it has to be simple. Its *integrity* has to be the same for the peasant as for the prince; for the Nobel prize-winner as for the educationally sub-normal; for the rural African in the Diocese of the Lundi as for the head of the transnational corporation who lives in Surrey. For it to be otherwise would mean that God is saying to those he has created: 'My gospel is not for you!'—and that is unthinkable. For what the gospel was to that first group of believers it can be to anyone, any time, anywhere.

The gospel is not a form of words, it is not a form of intellectual belief: it is a power and a presence that makes us right with God and establishes a relationship with God. Words and credal statements can be transmitted in numerous ways, but the power that is the Gospel has to be transmitted through converted people. For professing Christians, perhaps especially for those of us who earn our living by professing Christianity, it is a sobering thought that it is possible to be people 'holding to the outward form of godliness but denying its power' (2 Timothy 3:5, NRSV). Evangelism begins with personal conversion.

In this connection I was intrigued to hear from Archdeacon Junis Gwekwerere, whom I met in Zimbabwe recently, that he really came to know Jesus and was converted while he was priest in a remote area during the liberation war. The people were caught in the crossfire between Ian Smith's forces and the freedom fighters and were suffering terribly. His life was constantly in danger and the bishop asked him to leave. He refused. He could not see how the gospel could have any credibility with people who were trapped and dying in this way if he went away to save his own life and only returned afterwards when it became safe.

So he gave his wife and children the option of removing to safety, but they preferred to stay with him. Each night he went to bed he knew he might die at any moment. Every time he celebrated the Eucharist he knew it might be the last time. He knew there were eyes watching when he was visited by the security forces. He knew he was being watched by the security forces in case he should be visited by the freedom fighters. He knew that freedom fighters sometimes disguised themselves as security forces, and security forces personnel often disguised themselves as freedom fighters. He ministered to them all as occasions arose and not a hair of his head was harmed. He learnt then what living in Christ means. Yet he had been a priest for many years before that experience.

Last summer while on holiday I began to read the trilogy of church-centred novels by Susan Howatch. So I was fascinated to read in today's *Church Times* her account, told for the first time, of the religious conversion which she experienced seven years ago. She said there was no blinding light, no letters of fire in the sky, and certainly no choirs of angels singing 'welcome to the club'. She simply woke up one morning and realized that everything she had thought important was in fact unimportant, and everything she had thought unimportant was vital.

She was a successful, wealthy, best-selling novelist—a person with a glittering image. Then this power seized her and she knew that she had to uncover the unique personality blueprint God had given her and bring it to life, so that she could become the person he had designed her to be. So today she writes novels not in pursuit of fame and fortune but as an offering to God. It is not her job to worry about the ultimate purpose her books serve, or what that purpose is. Her job is to write the books as an offering to God so that he can use them as he thinks fit.

No one exemplifies the essence of evangelism better than St Paul. First, he has a personal story to tell—what he was, and what he is now. He did not change himself—he was changed by the power of God, and for him now every opportunity must be seized to share his good fortune with others. If you want a 'case study' for your 'evangelist's coaching manual' then read Acts 26, about Paul before King Agrippa.

Festus the Roman Governor of Caesarea was entertaining King Agrippa, and wanted a suitable state occasion to entertain him. Paul was a prisoner there waiting to be sent to Rome, so he was laid on to explain to Festus, King Agrippa and his wife Bernice and all the state officials who had assembled in great pomp, why the Jewish religious authorities wanted to kill him and what his offence was.

Paul knew the score. He knew this was not an occasion when people were enquiring into the Christian faith because they were seeking God. He knew he was there to entertain. But he forced them to take him seriously. He spoke without shame of his upbringing and his persecution of the followers of Jesus, and how he had come to the conviction that Jesus was the Christ and that Christ was for both Jew and Gentile.

First he is insulted. 'Festus shouted at him, "You are mad, Paul! Your great learning is driving you mad!"' But Paul keeps his cool. '"I am not mad, your Excellency! I am speaking the sober truth. King Agrippa! I can speak to you with all boldness, because you know about these things. I am sure that you have taken notice of every one of them, for this thing has not happened hidden away in a corner. King Agrippa, do you believe the prophets? I know that you do!"' (Acts 26:24–27, GNB). Then the embarrassed Agrippa attempts to evade Paul's direct challenge with flippancy. 'Looks as if you want to make me a Christian!' Still Paul is not deflected. 'Yes, I do. I want the whole world to share what I have—the good news of God's action in Christ.' (26:28–29, my paraphrase).

So Paul shows the way forward for us.

◆ *Seize every opportunity to tell the good news of Jesus, no matter how unpromising the situation may be.*

◆ *Be prepared to speak without shame about the errors and short-comings in our way of life before we stepped from that way into the way of Christ. In following Christ's way, doing the will of God is our first concern because God's action in Christ has made us what we now are.*

◆ *When patronized or insulted, refute it and say to ourselves, 'Keep your cool!'*

◆ *Be persistent—and don't let us be put off by flippancy or shallowness.*

◆ *Think about the total turnaround Paul had when he met the risen Christ—and reflect on what he said about it to King Agrippa.*

'I myself thought that I should do everything I could against the cause of Jesus of Nazareth. That is what I did in Jerusalem. I received authority from the chief priests and put many of God's people in prison; and when they were sentenced to death, I also voted against them. Many times I had them punished in the synagogues and tried to make them deny their faith. I was so furious with them that I even went to foreign cities to persecute them.

'It was for this purpose that I went to Damascus with authority and orders from the chief priests. It was on the road at midday, Your Majesty, that I saw a light much brighter than the sun, coming from the sky and shining round me and the men travelling with me. All of us fell to the ground, and I heard a voice say to me in Hebrew, "Saul, Saul! Why are you persecuting me? You are hurting yourself by hitting back, like an ox kicking against its owner's stick." "Who are you, Lord?" I asked. And the Lord answered, "I am Jesus, whom you persecute. But get up and stand on your feet. I have appeared to you to appoint you as my servant. You are to tell others what you have seen of me today and what I will show you in the future. I will rescue you from the people of Israel and from the Gentiles to whom I will send you. You are to open their eyes and turn them from the darkness to the light and from the power of Satan to God, so that through their faith in me they will have their sins forgiven and receive their place among God's chosen people."

'And so, King Agrippa, I did not disobey the vision I had from heaven. First in Damascus and in Jerusalem and then in all Judaea and among the Gentiles, I preached that they must repent of their sins and turn to God and do the things that would show that they had repented. It was for this reason that the Jews seized me while I was in the Temple, and they tried to kill me. But to this very day I have been helped by God, and so I stand here giving my witness to all, to small and great alike. What I say is the very same thing which the prophets and Moses said was going to happen: that the Messiah must suffer and be the first one to rise from death, to announce the light of salvation to the Jews and to the Gentiles.'

Acts 26:9–23 (GNB)

37

THE GOOD NEWS

Sermon preached by the Bishop of Croydon, the Right Revd Dr Wilfred Wood, at the Service of Welcome and Installation at Croydon Parish Church on Monday 16 September 1985

If a man shut his ears to the cry of the helpless, he will cry for help himself and not be heard.

Proverbs 21:13

Some months ago, one of our London Inner City priests suffered a burglary and his hi-fi equipment was stolen. When he went to buy a new hi-fi set he took one of his favourite records to try out the various sets on offer. He had heard this record many times and thought that he knew it well. But he was astounded to discover, as he played it on various pieces of equipment of the highest quality, that there were aspects of the music that he did not even know were present on the record. The music had always been present, but how much of it was heard and appreciated depended largely on the quality of the equipment through which it was heard.

This experience caused him to reflect upon the importance of the worshipping community—or church-goers if you prefer—in any particular place. God, through his Holy Spirt, is present everywhere in the world he created, and some nineteen hundred years ago he became visible to human eyes in the person of Jesus Christ. Ordinary human beings were given access to the mind of God, as Jesus, by word and action expressed that mind on the social, economic, political and religious issues of the day. Today, that same Jesus is just as truly present in the community of baptized persons we call the Church. He is present in all his fulness just as the music was fully present on the record. But the Church is the medium by which men and women will see him and respond to him, and it is therefore the quality of the Church's life and witness which will determine how much of Jesus men and women see, and on which they will make their response to him. After all, it is still true that 'greater faith hath no man than the bald-headed man who buys hair restorer from a bald-headed pharmacist!' What Christians *are* and *do* will always be more important to non-believers than what we say.

There is a most instructive incident recorded in Luke 18:35–43. It was the custom, in the time of Christ, for devout Jews to make a yearly pilgrimage to Jerusalem to celebrate the Passover Festival. Groups of pilgrims could be seen travelling on foot, and, as they passed through the various villages, those people, who for one reason or another could not make the pilgrimage, would line the route to greet them and wish them Godspeed. On this occasion Jesus and his disciples were on pilgrimage and, as was his custom, Jesus spoke to his companions and others around him as he walked along. Near Jericho there was a blind wayside beggar who heard the commotion and asked what was going on. When told that it was Jesus who was passing he began to shout out, 'Jesus, Jesus, take pity on me!' The people round Jesus told the beggar to shut up, but he persisted. Jesus stopped and asked the crowd to let the blind man through. He asked the blind man what he wanted, and he replied that he wanted his sight back. Jesus said to him, 'Receive your sight', and from then on he was able to see.

I have always been intrigued by the behaviour of the people around Jesus, some of whom must have been his close disciples. Why were they trying to silence the blind beggar? Did they see it as their job to keep Jesus respectable? To protect him from damaging association with non-respectable people such as beggars, cripples and the like?

Or were they concerned to keep Jesus to themselves? They certainly wanted to hear him, to learn from him, to be entertained by him—but for their own benefit, not anybody else's. So they were protective.

And from where he stood, what did the blind beggar perceive? He heard a group of people who surrounded Jesus, but *their* very nearness to Jesus was keeping him away.

There are many, many lessons to be learnt from this story. The most important is that above all the clamour, and in spite of the efforts of the people around him, Jesus was still able to hear the poor man's cry. Jesus always hears the cries of those who are helpless and oppressed and he is continually saying: 'Let them through, let them through, let them through.'

The second discovery is that when we listen to the cries of those who are pushed aside, we learn that they want no more than what the rest of us take for granted. The blind beggar wanted no more than to be able to see—just like everyone else.

The Christian community in any place—and the Croydon Episcopal Area is no exception—must continually ask itself, as it walks along with Jesus, if its own nearness to Jesus is precisely what is keeping away those in greatest need. Because it is possible to claim the name of Jesus, to walk with him, to hear him speak, to be entertained by him, to enjoy his company, and yet not share his concern for those who are losers in the rat race of life.

And yet it is upon this that all else depends. Because prophecy, evangelism, mission and any other laudable concern we may wish the Church to engage in *must come out of pastoral concern. The Incarnation was the greatest pastoral act of all time.* That is to say that just as Jesus was taken up with those who were left behind, discarded or pushed into the hedgerows of life, and made them *his* first concern, so people will see Jesus in the worshipping community when that community clearly demonstrates that whatever may be prevalent attitudes in state or nation, for the *Christian community* the men and women who are at the bottom of society's pile are at the top of the Church's list. If we move away from this central concern of Jesus, then church life at best will be no more than a tolerable harmless cultural diversion, our church buildings no more than places for inexpensive entertainment, and the mouthings of our clergy like that schoolteacher who showed his class the same film over and over again, and sometimes to vary the routine he ran it backwards!

But we must *not* move from this central concern of Jesus. We will find that this concern is not at all in keeping with the prevailing attitudes around us where today great emphasis is placed on the acquisition of industrial wealth, status and power. We will need to remember that it was also like this in Jesus' day. What he did in his teaching, and by his actions, was to point to the kingdom of God; to show up the ugly difference between the way his listeners were living in the sinful and corrupt values of their time, and his vision of a kingdom where love, justice, mercy and hope were dominant. He challenged his hearers to step out of their situation and into the reality he was describing.

The challenge of Jesus to his hearers *then* is his challenge to us now—to those of us who are near enough to hear his voice. And because we all watch television and read newspapers, we who are walking along with Jesus will know that the cry for help rising above the clamour of our domestic concerns is coming not from a blind wayside beggar, but from black people in Soweto, Sharpeville and elsewhere.

When I was a boy at primary school in Barbados, playground bullies had an infallible method of picking a fight with a victim. They would draw a circle on the ground around the spot on which the victim was standing, and then inform him that if he stepped out of that circle he was attacking them. To be born black in South Africa is to be born within a circle drawn by a ruling racist *régime*—not 'government', because a government derives its just powers from the consent of those who are governed.

Within that circle, your parents may not be accorded the respect and dignity of homemakers. They may not choose where they may live or work, the better to discharge their responsibilities to you, their child. They may not choose for you the school most likely to draw out your God-given gifts to fit you for service for humankind; they may not seek to change their station in life by peaceful means by voting for law-makers who would make more humane laws, because they are not allowed to vote. By protesting about these conditions you and your parents are breaking the law and are accordingly beaten with whips, tortured in prison and sometimes shot.

To be born black in South Africa is to cry to Jesus for help; to hear him surrounded by Christians in this country and elsewhere who ask you to be quiet because they value the friendship of your racist oppressors. When will such Christians listen instead to Jesus and hear him say: 'Let him through, let him through, let him through'?

In our Croydon Episcopal Area, we will be for and against the Bishop of Durham; for and against the ordination of women; for and against every contemporary preoccupation of today's Church. We will strive to make liturgy expressive, and our worship enjoyable; we will play our part in the life of our various communities; we will proclaim that we are an Easter people and Alleluia is our song. But we will not forget that at the heart of our faith is a man on a cross—someone whom we profess to love because he first loved us. He it is who nourishes us in word and sacrament with his body and blood. But he is there because his concern first and last was with those who were helpless and left behind. This too must be our concern and out of this, with his help, will come prophetic witness, evangelism and mission, all of which are so necessary for the advancement of the kingdom in this place.

Bible reading notes from BRF

BRF publishes two regular series of Bible reading notes—*New Daylight* and *Guidelines*. These are published three times a year (in January, May and September).

New Daylight provides a pattern for daily Bible reading. Each day's reading contains a Bible passage (printed out in full, from the version chosen by the contributor), along with a brief commentary and explanation, and a suggestion for prayer, meditation or reflection. The sections of commentary often draw on and reflect the experiences of the contributors themselves and thus offer contemporary and personal insights into the readings. Sunday readings focus on the themes of prayer and Holy Communion.

Guidelines contains running commentary, with introductions and background information, arranged in weekly units. Each week's material is usually broken up into at least six sections. Readers can take as much or as little at a time as they wish. The whole 'week' can be used at a sitting, or split up into convenient parts: this flexible arrangement allows for one section to be used each weekday. A Bible will be needed. The last section of each week is usually called 'Guidelines' and has points for thought, meditation and prayer. A short list of books, to help with further reading, appears at the end of some contributions.

Both *New Daylight* and *Guidelines* may be obtained from your local Christian bookshop or by subscription direct from BRF.

For more information about the notes and the full range of BRF publications, write to: BRF, Peter's Way, Sandy Lane West, OXFORD, OX4 5HG (Tel: 0865 748227)